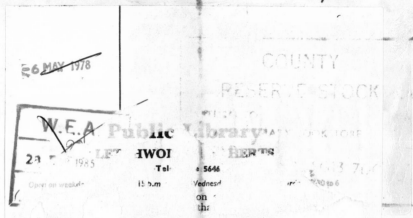

The changing
form of fashion

The changing form of fashion

Madge Garland

J. M. Dent & Sons Limited London

First published 1970
© Madge Garland, 1970

Printed in Great Britain by
W. P. Griffith & Sons Limited London & Bedford
for J. M. Dent & Sons Limited
Aldine House Bedford Street London

ISBN 0 460 03799 4

Contents

List of plates

Introduction

No animal attempts to alter its natural shape; man does. The lion wears his mane, the zebra his stripes, the giraffe his neck unselfconsciously, but man has never been satisfied with himself and wishes to improve his appearance.

In pre-war museums immense galleries, dauntingly marked 'Ethnography', were filled to overflowing with the dusty artefacts of early man which his civilized descendants had gathered together in the search for their origins. Now, displayed with more discernment and with many of the exhibits transferred to 'art' departments and others to 'costume' all, however classified, illustrate man's desire to improve on nature. The North American Indians compressed their infants' soft skulls, the Chinese bound the feet of their female children, western women constricted their waists, though few transformations were as extreme as man's attempt to change the human physiognomy into that of an animal, so horribly and brilliantly illustrated by Charles Lebrun in the mid seventeenth century.

The whole subject of the artificial means whereby the human frame can be altered belongs to anthropology rather than to fashion, yet this passion for improvement – or at any rate for change – lies behind all the whims of fashion throughout centuries.

One of the earliest and most universal attempts to change the body's shape was to alter what appears to be the least tractable

and most precious portion – the cranium. An elongated or
wedge-shaped head has always been considered desirable
and the epithet 'roundhead' appears to have been as
uncomplimentary to the Chinook Indians as to the Royalist
English of the seventeenth century, though the latter merely
scoffed at the closely cropped hair of their Parliamentary
opponents while the Indians actually flattened their children's
heads by means of a plank tied down to the piece of wood on
which the unfortunate infant was strapped. This was only one
of many means used by various races at different times
throughout the world, and in the past mothers spared
themselves no trouble and their children no pain in an
endeavour to give them a fashionable shape.

Skull deformations are mentioned by Herodotus, Hippocrates
and Strabo; they were practised by the ancient Egyptians and
by certain sects of Chinese priests until the eighteenth century,
lingered on in some remote French provinces until the
nineteenth, and African babies with bound heads have been
photographed in comparatively recent years. The admiration
for an elongated cranium still has its followers and a few years
ago the use of hair-pads and back-combing were popular
methods of making the back of the head appear higher than
the forehead.

A long neck is another coveted beauty attribute admired in
both sexes and all continents. Western women have merely
agreed it to be a sign of beauty sung by their poets and
accentuated by their painters, but Eastern women have gone
about acquiring it by forceful means. In Burma the Padaung
tribe encircle the women's necks with heavy metal rings,
adding one after another until the vertebrae separate so that, if
the rings were removed, the head would wobble on the
shoulders. Some Negroes of the Ivory Coast used cord collars
to achieve the same result and the bronze figures of Sardinian
warriors have equally high necklaces of somewhat similar
design, but in most European countries men and women have
contented themselves by simulating a long neck with boned or
stiffened collars.

The preference for small feet reached its most exaggerated
form in the stunted feet of the pre-Revolution upper-class

Chinese women. The nearest approach to this in the west was the fashion for shoes with stiletto heels and pointed toes of the early 1960s.

Hideous lip-mutilations were as common in northern Alaska as in tropical Africa, where it was the custom of certain tribes to enlarge the lower lip until it jutted out like a duck's bill. In the Western world enlarged lips were fashionable in the 1930s but achieved by less painful methods: Joan Crawford's impressive mouth owed much to dark red lipstick. When it is fashionable for lips to be only a pale glimmer it would be as rude to accentuate a mouth as in former times it would have been to show a foot. Examples of ear-mutilations can be found all over the world and of all the various alterations once made to lips, ears, nose and cheeks, the perforated ear-lobe ready to receive an earring is the last survival.

Today we dress first and add our jewellery later but, historically speaking, accessories came first and clothing developed from ornament, not vice versa. Body decoration was among man's earliest aesthetic activities and represents one of his first attempts to assert his superiority over the animal world around him. It antedates clothing by many hundreds of years, just as clothes antedate the creation of a house. Fashion is by far the oldest of the arts and man was interested in adorning his body long before he considered sheltering it from the elements.

Early explorers are unanimous in their astonishment at such peoples as the Fuegians and the Patagonians, the one inhabiting an island swept by harsh winds, the other living in a severe highland climate, who dressed themselves only in painted stripes and spots. Nor did the inhabitants of the Marquesas develop any shield against the tropical sun of their Pacific islands other than the complicated patterns with which they painted themselves from head to foot. The Pictish women seemed oblivious of their country's cold climate, and proud of the blue stars and decorative arabesques of their body painting, if we can credit John White's drawings of them. In ancient Britain the girls stained themselves all over with a brownish lotion which must have given a somewhat similar effect to an application of artificial suntan.

The Australian aborigines, like all primitive people, have

always been inveterate painters and consider the materials for their art of such importance that they make expeditions, sometimes lasting several months, for no other reason than to obtain the required unguents. As Captain Cook put it: 'The native was content to be naked but ambitious to be fine.' Fine they certainly are, and the elaborate designs carried out on their bodies in pipe-clay, red ochre, yellow and black are very similar to contemporary abstract paintings.

Depilation was also widely practised and is quite common today, though not as much in vogue as in the sixteenth century, when women plucked the hair from their foreheads in order to make the latter appear very high, or in the 1920s when eye-brows were plucked out completely and replaced by lines drawn in at an unnatural angle.

All the important events of primitive man's life, initiation, war, courtship, marriage and death, were occasions for special body decorations just as, on a diminishing scale, they are occasions for special clothes today. The love of dressing-up is born in every child, most little boys attempt to extend the possibilities of their small persons with cowboy hats, Red Indian feathers or spacemen's helmets. The conduct of everyday people when 'dressed up' or in fancy dress is quite other than their normal procedure and their state of mind is conditioned by their awareness of their different appearance. An extra dimension is envisaged and explored which helps to develop the personality, and can in some instances alter it. To be able to change one's identity as well as one's appearance is a basic human wish, as much desired by the woman of fashion as by the initiate of a religion.

Today's dressing-up which teams an Edwardian feather boa with a trouser suit, or a beaded chiffon dress of the 1920s with a leather coat is a gesture of defiance to a world of increasing conformity.

Man has never been a diffident dresser: he has painted his body intricately from top to toe, adorned it with feathers, dressed it in furs, learnt to create the most elaborate clothes for the beautification of his person and has often spent as much as a quarter of his waking time on this planet altering, decorating and dressing up his meagre form. Lord Chesterfield when giving advice to his son in the eighteenth century pointed out that dress was one of the ingredients of the art of pleasing and 'therefore an object of some attention', adding 'there is infinitely more wisdom in submitting to than in spurning those necessary concomitants of civilization, which being artificial throughout, require the cement of elegance and refinement of polish.' Yet in spite of such sponsors and the antiquity of its lineage there has always been a faintly derogatory attitude towards fashion on the part of the intellectuals, and a slightly defensive manner in those who deal in it. Could this be because the tailor is not among the workers mentioned in the Scriptures? The trousered barbarians, Scythians or Saxons, have been contrasted with the civilized Greeks wearing draped chlamys and tunic held together by golden pin or girdle, but innocent of the tailor's skill. The legend of the gentle savage who knew of no changing fashions persisted until the late nineteenth century when, as more and more became known about our primitive forbears, it was discovered that they too, even if fashion consisted only of a feather or some fancy body-paintings, were also fashion-conscious and managed to be just as sinful and warlike as their civilized descendants without the excuse of seams and sewing.

Herbert Read once remarked that the English were not an artistic race but that they could not avoid art. The same may be said of fashion. Most English people are (or were) conservative and recoil with distaste from each new style. Nevertheless, though they may adopt it reluctantly, the shape of their clothes is dictated by their epoch. Even dress-reformers such as Mrs Amelia Jenks Bloomer wore clothes belonging palpably to their own time.

In the past there were recognized types of clothing which clearly proclaimed the wearer as rich or poor, a virgin, married woman or old lady, and each state had its concomitant responsibilities and privileges. Now a fear both of class-consciousness and of age-classification becomes more and more noticeable as the decades pass and today's clothes no longer mark the position or occupation of the wearer. Mothers and daughters dress in the same casual clothes and, whereas children were once dressed as miniature adults, today grown women are dressed as outsize children. Some special events still usher in special costumes: a bride's dress, a court ceremonial, an opening of Parliament, a Lord Mayor's banquet – these are the last remnants of a dying tradition. We seem, sartorially speaking, if in no other way, to be approaching More's Utopia in which no distinction of dress was to be permitted.

1 Shape

As soon as primitive man had learned to weave and could
produce fabrics in which to clothe himself, he began to
experiment with the different shapes made possible by his
garments. Now not only could he alter the shape of his head,
neck, nose, ears and feet by slow and painful methods but could
immediately contrive a totally different appearance by changing
the form of his costume. He has been doing this ever since and
has called this activity 'fashion'.

Fashion in the sense of costume is said to have its origin in
many different sources: in sex attraction, in a sense of possession
and love of display, in modesty, as a totem representing
magical powers or as a protection against the elements. In
China and Greece it was long believed that costume had
developed as a protection, and to intelligent and civilized
peoples such as the Chinese and the Greeks it must have
seemed only reasonable that clothes should have been made to
protect the sensitive human body from the extremes of climate.

Most modern psychoanalysts, ethnographers, and even the
Bible, disagree with the rational idea of necessity and maintain
that dress is a direct descendant of magic, a sign of majesty and
power. Clothes are for dignity and adornment, not for
protection, and the annals of fashion history are not concerned
with modesty or practical merit, but with power-consciousness
and aesthetics. The shape of the human body is evidently not

immutable, but changes in some way with each civilization and way of life. The ideal beauty of body in Phidias' day is unlike that of our present time; the elongated grace of Jean Goujon's sixteenth-century statues contrasts strongly with the splendid women painted by Rubens, who again are totally different from the plump and dimpled courtesans of Boucher's canvases. Ingres with painstaking care reconstructed a girl's body in antiquity; today Bernard Buffet's emaciated and disillusioned women are among the few illustrations of femininity recorded. In the twentieth century humanity appears to have come to terms with being a 'naked ape' and is content to clothe but not to deform its body.

In the past man's dissatisfaction with nature's mass production of one torso, two arms and two legs, all of much the same shape and size, has led him to invent a myriad variations and with the aid of whalebone, wood, canvas, starch and stuffing he has widened the hips with bolsters, wooden hoops or bombasted breeches, produced the effect of hypertrophy of the buttocks and increased the rotundity of the bosom by pads, made military the shoulders with epaulettes, enlarged the arms with monstrous sausages or leg-o'-mutton sleeves, divorced the head from the body by huge ruffs and, above all, pulled in the waist.

The natural shape of the female body has not been revealed and free as it is today for fifteen hundred years, when girls played games in bikinis identical to those now worn, as the mosaic pavement of the Piazza Armerina in Sicily clearly shows, and according to a 300 B.C. bronze statue, girl runners wore short shifts strikingly like mini skirts. These are exceptions, and for most of the time the constriction of the waist and the expansion of the bosom have been two of fashion's main themes for women. The slender figure now admired would have been cause for pity before the First World War when lovely women were expected to have fine shoulders, a large bust and rounded hips. Until recently excessive fattening of young girls was part of the ritual which preceded marriage in some tribes in Africa, just as nowadays girls in Europe take a slimming course before a bathing holiday.

The present silhouette is one which cannot be achieved by

any extraneous means; the body itself must be exactly right and to maintain or obtain the measurements now considered attractive thousands of women are willing to undergo courses of near-starvation, brutal pommelling and boring exercises.

The human being's obsession with his shape is clearly shown in the earliest known prehistoric drawings and artefacts: what primitive man wanted most, and therefore admired most, was the fertility upon which his survival depended, and early representations of the female form were almost certainly connected with the concept of fertility. The Venus of Willendorf, the Venus of Lespugne, the Sleeping Woman of Gozo, and the early Hittite figurines, all discovered in this century, show female figures small in actual scale but immensely corpulent in form. The paleolithic Venus of Willendorf, composed of limestone still bearing traces of red paint, is only 4½ inches high but has huge buttocks, breasts and a swollen stomach; the standing ivory figure of the Venus of Lespugne shows even greater stylized corpulence with protruding buttocks; and the neolithic Maltese figures, thought to be connected with the Temple of Sleep or the Incubation, are of reclining women whose huge circumference is composed of balloon-like skirts ending in pleated flounces.

In sharp contradiction to the corpulent figures, though also belonging to pre-history and tentatively dated in the third millennium B.C., are the highly stylized 'fiddle' figures, so called because of their strange shape, found in the Eastern Mediterranean, Anatolia and Cyprus. These little figures, usually carved from flattened discs of marble with the head and arms reduced to long vertical projections, were scarcely known in the west when Brancusi sculpted such abstractions as his marble head now in New York's Museum of Modern Art, which closely resembles the pre-history figurines in its economy of design.

The earliest known representation in the world of a slender female figure and possibly one of its first pictures is the White Lady of the Brandberg massif in South West Africa with its long limbs and exaggeratedly thin body. The paper-thin elegance of the bird-headed goddesses of Jabbaren in the Upper Nile, tentatively dated in the eighteenth dynasty, recall the

1920s' idea of beauty, for the Egyptians obviously admired slender figures and their tomb paintings and carved reliefs show women wearing narrow, ankle-length skirts tied beneath small breasts.

Some thousands of years later than the 'fiddle' figures but almost equally abstract are the Etruscan bronzes. One now in the Louvre shows an immensely tall thin stele with a female head and well modelled features, but with the limbs barely suggested, which has a curious affinity to Giacometti's Striding Man and other elongated figures sculptured by him in the 1950s. More often it was the curvaceous figure which was admired, and it was not until mankind became appalled at the idea of over-population and attempted by various means to reduce the birth-rate that excessive thinness was considered beautiful. It is significant that in the 1920s, when birth control was first generally practised (but only in the upper strata of society, those that needed it most having neither knowledge nor opportunity to plan their families) the boyish female figure was popular. Now when 'the pill' is a subject of general conversation and an appallingly high birth-rate threatens to swamp the world, the androgynous figure of Twiggy has appeared which makes the 'flapper' of the 1920s appear comparatively womanly. Even during these periods man now and again has protested against such an artificial standard, has recalled his early love of the large fecund woman and in spite of all the accepted canons of taste has admired Mae West's bust and hips when neither was in fashion, or made Jayne Mansfield's outsize bosom an outsize box-office draw. But neither was emulated by her own sex in either generation: they were lone exceptions created for and by basic masculine desires and scorned by their more fashion-conscious female contemporaries.

Between the extremes of these two ideals, the grotesquely fat and the abstractly thin, human taste has vacillated through the ages.

J. B. S. Haldane once pointed out that four of the most important biological inventions in the life of man were made before the dawn of history. He lists them as the domestication of animals, of plants, and of the fungi for producing alcohol, but considers the fourth of more 'ultimate and far-reaching importance than any of these, since it altered the path of sexual selection, focused the attention of man as a lover upon women's face and breasts, and changed our idea of beauty from the steatopygous Hottentot to the modern European, from the Venus of Brassempouy to the Venus de Milo' though, of course, 'there are certain races which have not yet taken this last step'. This idea does much to explain the ambivalence of man's feelings towards women which have ranged from early fertility fetichism, the worship of a pure and robed Madonna and the desire for a half-naked vamp. The first concept fades away in pre-history but the other two have disputed men's love and women's attention throughout history. Sometimes fashion has favoured one, sometimes the other.

Although standards of taste change perpetually, there are certain canons of beauty which recur more often than others and admiration for a small waist is widespread and frequent. Even when it is ignored, as it was by the charming Tanagra figures of 300 B.C., by the *Merveilleuses* of the Directoire in their transparent muslins or by the flappers of the 1920s in their shapeless *crêpe-de-Chine* slips, the half-hidden waist was expected to be small. In *Tales from the Arabian Nights* there are many descriptions of the voluptuous forms of the houris, the great temples of Thailand and India are carved with myriads of apsaras and goddesses, all of whom show large bosoms and buttocks, but all have small waists. No poet ever sang the width and breadth of his loved one's thick waist and even the Muslim when praising the beauties of large swaying buttocks described these mounds of pleasure as joined to swelling bosoms by a waist 'so slight that the sun can cast no shadow'.

The earliest known example of a corset is to be seen in the 4,000-year-old frescoes of the palace of Minos at Knossos. Both men and women are portrayed wearing corsets, the court ladies dressed in tight bodices and ground-length flounced skirts which give them much the same silhouette as a mid-Victorian lady. Whalebone and even iron was used for corsets, and a terrifying example of the latter material, dated as late as the sixteenth century, can be seen in the Musée de Cluny. Most peasants used leather corsets and the Circassians,

who attached extreme importance to a wasp-waist, bound
their girl children's bodies with leather which was not removed
until their wedding night. An English ladies' magazine of the
mid nineteenth century advocated much the same procedure.
It stressed the difficulties a grown girl might find in lacing her
waist to the fashionable size if precautions had not been taken
earlier, pointing out that if a corset was put on at an early
age the figure could be gradually moulded by it; if at the age
of 14 the waist was still too large, a smaller size of corset
should be worn and pulled in until the requisite slimness was
achieved. No wonder a Victorian doctor when asked what
was the matter with a fashionable patient who complained of
internal pains replied: 'Your corset, damn it!'

With a few exceptions the nipped-in waist had its most
extreme expression in the north and played little part in the
sunny Mediterranean world. The Dorian chiton, such as those
worn by the maidens in sculptures on the Acropolis in
Athens, was fastened by a simple pin and often left open on
one side. The long chiton, or tunic, which passed from
Assyria by way of the Phoenicians to the Asiatic side of the
Aegean and so to Greece, is not found in prehistoric art and
is of a later date than the short woollen tunic preferred in
Homer's day. Underclothing was scanty and consisted of a
light, sleeveless under-tunic and a fascia or brassière, and an
outer tunic known as a stola or palla. None of these classic
styles accentuated the waist and they continued to be worn
from the first century B.C. to the second century A.D. with
little change in cut, but with different colours and decorations
to give variety, of which there appeared to be plenty since a
carping Roman critic exclaimed: 'What are they at, sir, these
women that invent new names for garments every year? The
Loose-knit tunic, the Close-knit tunic, the Linenblue, the
Interior, the Goldedge, the Marigold or Crocus tunic, the
shift — or Shiftless — the Mantilla, the Royal or Exotic, the
Wavy or the Downy, the Nutty or the Waxy — not a kernel of
sense in all of it!'

Great fashion changes usually come about through great
political and social upheavals; in a static society dress tends to
change but little. During the long centuries of the ancient

empires of China and Egypt fashion remained remarkably
stable, but with wars and conquests, new markets for home
goods are opened up, new ideas come from abroad, commercial
treaties alter the respective values of basic materials, make the
fortune of some and ruin others, royal marriages introduce
foreign fashions which are adopted by the court and later
infiltrate down to the wealthy burghers. Kings, queens and
courtesans have played the roles now undertaken by professional
models and the medium of advertising in the promotion of
new fashions. Events of major importance, such as Napoleon's
victories in Italy and his attempted conquest of Egypt, brought
about the revival of a pseudo-classical-cum-Egyptian style —
but for ladies only. The basic fashion for men remained
virtually the same as it had been ever since the Roman toga
was discarded for the trousers which originally came into
Europe when Scythian horsemen over-rode Thrace.

The classic idea of moderation, nothing too much, nothing
too little, disappeared under voluminous garments of Byzantine
inspiration and for centuries the human body was invisible
beneath multifarious robes and mantles.

The Normans adopted these fashions through their contacts
with Byzantine civilization in south Italy and they were later
diffused throughout southern Europe, mainly through the
Angevin court at Naples. Many Byzantine princesses married
into the Western courts, and an English woman of high rank in
the twelfth century was scarcely distinguishable from a lady of
the Eastern Empire.

Edward III is credited with being the king who taught the
English people how to dress, but there were several reasons
why style and quality of clothing improved greatly during his
reign, chief among them the increase of the wool trade with
the Continent which brought a considerable amount of money
into England. Old men continued to wear long mantles but
by the middle of the fourteenth century the usual male dress
was short-skirted and as simple as it was elegant, consisting
of tights and a slightly fitted tunic which reached to mid-thigh,
a costume curiously similar to the attire of Etruscan men some
900 years previously and to the mini-shift-dress of English
girls some 600 years later.

True tailoring begins in England in the fourteenth century, for although the first recorded tailor's name is that of Baldwin who settled in England under William II and is credited with making great improvements in fabrics, there is little evidence of the tailoring craft until this time. A ballad of that date addressed to tailors describes them as gods 'who can transform an old garment into the shape of a new one', and there was every need of their ingenuity for the change in dress was fundamental. The tailor's dream of many seams but no creases replaced the dressmaker's idea of few seams and many folds, and a definite division was recognized between draped garments and those in which the material was cut, shaped by seams and then stitched together. Innumerable variations can be achieved with both methods, though the latter offers more scope and has been the only known form of dress in Western Europe since the collapse of the Roman Empire.

In the early sixteenth century it was the men who made the chief fashion news while women continued to be covered up to the chin and down to the ground, and it is noteworthy that the period of the troubadours in Europe and the Courts of Love in France coincides with the time when women were mysteriously concealed beneath coifs, trailing sleeves and long robes.

On the rare occasions when the nude is portrayed in medieval illustrations a strange sway-back is revealed together with low buttocks and swelling bellies but with small, high-placed breasts, such as the Master of Niederheim shows in his illustration of *The Charm of Love*. Only Cranach has succeeded in making this type attractive; the Dürer nudes and the three contestants in the anonymous *Judgment of Paris* at Basle have heavy torsos, pronounced buttocks and large feet which would not get them into the first round of any provincial beauty contest today.

The figure-fitting gown was the forerunner of the corset which became firmly established at the beginning of the sixteenth century and from then on, although it has appeared in a number of different shapes, it never went out of fashion until the 1920s. It is known that many women like the feeling of being firmly encased and it was once thought that 'tight-lacing kindles impure desires'. If this is so, it must be responsible for a great deal of mischief because, except for the *Merveilleuses* of the Directoire, no one attempted to do without a corset until the famous dressmaker Paul Poiret denounced it before the First World War. He forbade his lovely wife Denise to wear one, but his clients were less co-operative and it was not until more than a decade later that the corset was banished by the flappers of the 1920s who equated it with the old-fashioned propriety they were intent on repudiating.

The early sixteenth-century corset was usually of leather which gave the upholstered look characteristic of the period, a bulkiness in part due to the current fashion for material being used on the straight and gathered, whereas medieval robes were often cut on the cross and therefore more flowing.

The straight gathered skirt and tight-fitting bodice of this period became the prototype of peasant costumes all over Europe, which varied in detail from one locality to another. A rising oval *décolletage* was typical of the mid sixteenth century, exquisitely recorded by Corneille de Lyon and by Clouet in his portrait of Elizabeth of Austria, Queen of France, where she wears a puffed and jewelled yoke, the high oval neckline outlined with jewels and knots of pearls, and a small lace-edged ruff. In all these dresses the waist was firmly fitted at the natural line, the bodice revealed the curve of the bosom, and the slightly stiffened skirt swelled out until it reached the ground.

For a time the area controlled by the corset was extended to include both the upper and lower part of the body and this led to the curious shape so well illustrated in Holbein's portrait of Anne Cresacres, who in 1527 was betrothed to John, the only son of Sir Thomas More, in which a flat-chested bodice is continued into a forward-slanting stomach.

The forward-slanting stomach can be seen again in seventeenth-century Flemish paintings, and appeared again in the 1950s when it amused the young models, who had never worn a boned garment, to assume such a posture.

Women outdid themselves in the sixteenth century in producing such monstrosities as the farthingale, a ludicrous shape supposed to have originated in the amours and consequent pregnancy of an important lady which had to be kept secret and was sometimes called a *garde-enfant*. Certainly the east-to-west width of a Spanish farthingale could easily hide both lover and child beneath its capacious frame. The French favoured 'whalebone wheels that shelter all defects from head to heels' supported by a bolster tied round the hips beneath the 'wheel' and above covered by a frill, with a gathered skirt falling from the perimeter of the circle. In England during Elizabeth I's reign the women's straight-fronted corsets of whalebone and leather ended in a point below the stomach and to this foundation was fixed a horizontal shelf encircling the body, usually wider at the sides than at the front or back, over which the skirt was draped and gathered. This, together with enormous sleeves, composed one of the most extraordinary and unnatural shapes which man's ingenuity has ever devised. In the many portraits of Queen Elizabeth I, when she is seen half or three-quarter length, the extreme beauty of the elaborate materials and the exquisite detail of the embroidery and jewellery enchant the eye and the foreshortening of the figure is not visible, but full-length pictures, such as that of 1588 by Crespin de Passe, which shows her returning from a thanks-giving for the defeat of the Spanish Armada, exhibits only too clearly the unfortunate proportions, made worse by the comparatively short skirts which revealed the feet and the high collar which obscured the neckline. Short-legged, long-bodied, the natural beauty of waist, breast and hips obliterated, Elizabeth, covered in jewels, resembled an oriental idol rather than a Christian queen. So remote was the total effect from any natural form that it is no wonder women appeared to Philip Stubbs not to be 'fleshe and blood but rather puppits or mawmets consisting of rags and clouts compact together', except that the 'rags and clouts' were of magnificent brocades, velvets and jewel-embroidered silks.

The huge sixteenth-century ruffs totally divorced the head from the body, and presented it as if served up on a platter of pleated and starched linen. The art of dealing with 'cabage ruffes of outrageous size, Starched in colour to beholders' eyes'

which reached their maximum size around 1580 was part of
every well brought-up girl's education, and a Flemish woman,
Frau Dingham van der Plafze, who came to London to teach
this art, charged five pounds for a course of lessons and an
extra pound for giving the recipe of how to make the starch.

Another form of sixteenth-century neckwear was a high collar
called a 'medici' after Marie de Medici. This made a becoming
background to the face and allowed a necklace to be worn on
the bare neck in front, a fashion Elizabeth I often favoured and
to which she sometimes added two immense wings wired out
from the shoulders which still further accentuated a distressingly
ill-proportioned figure. In spite of all this finery she insisted on
home-made articles and denounced imported ruffs and cloaks,
calling on both sexes to 'leave off such fine disguises and
monstrous manner of attiring themselves, as are insupportable
for charges and indecent to be worn' which seem harsh words
from a woman who left over 1,000 items of clothing including
wraps and three coronation robes: the red velvet in which she
drove to the Abbey, the gold tissue in which she was crowned
and the purple velvet which she put on afterwards. But she did
make one economy: she continued to wear the red velvet
gown for the opening of Parliament and her large wardrobe
appears modest compared with Catherine of Russia's which, in
1761, according to the *Correspondance Secrète de Métra,*
contained 8,700 complete costumes.

An equally unfortunate combination of a high head-dress
with enlarged hips and a skirt short enough to show the feet
occurred again in the 1780s when preposterous head-dresses rose
two feet above the head and hooped skirts barely reached the
ankles, thus placing the head only marginally above the central
line of the body and throwing the whole figure out of scale.

The wife of James I, Anne of Denmark, showed her
natural bad taste in monstrous farthingales, high behind and
low before, which got stuck in the passages so often that the
king issued a proclamation against ladies wearing them, of
which no notice was taken; skirts continued to swell,
though the full size was seen only on formal occasions, and for
shopping in town smaller hoops were worn under the
petticoats, which sometimes were so long that they trailed on

the ground. Eventually the farthingale was discarded, but by this time James was dead.

An immense change came over the silhouette with the accession of Charles I and his consort Henrietta Maria, often referred to as the founder of good taste in England. The ruff, the Marie Stuart cap and the farthingale disappeared, the bodice ended at the natural waist, which was fitted but not unduly corseted, full sleeves gathered at the elbow or wrist were often drawn in at the centre to form two puffs but were not stiffened, the moderate *décolletage* was softened by lace or a collar, full skirts reached the ground and hid the feet. Unpatterned materials, fine laces and few jewels composed a style of rich elegance as different in shape as in detail from the Tudor's magnificent elaboration.

At the Restoration women's shape changed very little but poor Catherine of Braganza when she arrived from Portugal to marry Charles II was still wearing the long-outmoded farthingale which she soon abandoned for English dress, though she fought to keep her skirts shorter than the English ladies because she was proud of her small feet – alas, her only claim to beauty.

King Charles's mistresses quite often dispensed with their corsets and in pictures by Lely and Mignard they are seen *en déshabille,* their careless ringlets and satin *négligées* in strong contrast to the ladies in stark ruffs, rigid stomachers and huge farthingales with which the century had begun. Although the full bosoms of the favourites, Louise de Kéroualle, Barbara Villiers and Hortense Mancini, are clearly displayed in their portraits, when Lely painted 'Sweet Nell' naked, a picture said to have been hidden in Charles's room behind another less provocative one, it showed a slender girl with a delicately rounded body.

Most women, however, continued to be tightly laced, but the late seventeenth-century corset changed its line and, instead of the straight profile of an Elizabethan body, it compressed the upper bust and once more gave the stomach a slight forward slant, somewhat like a modified version of the protruding bellies of ladies during the Middle Ages.

This was followed by another new shape and Fielding

speaks of 'slender young women who seem rather intended to
hang up in the hall of an anatomist than for any other purpose'.
It was generally agreed that 'no woman could be genteel who
is not flat before', and to make sure girls held themselves
upright, knitting needles were put down the front of their
bodices which would stab them in the chin if they drooped
forward over their writing or sewing. With these flat stiff
bodices, such as one sees in portraits by Devis, hoops continued
to be worn and in 1711 Sir Roger de Coverley described the
variations through which the hoop had passed in three
generations: 'My great-great-grandmother has on the new-
fashioned petticoat, except that the modern is gathered at the
waist; my grandmother appears as if she stood in a large drum,
whereas the ladies now walk as if they were in a go-cart'. The
'large drum' was the farthingale of James I, the new-fashioned
one widened gradually from the waist to the ground, concealing
the feet, and had an overskirt looped up round the hips, falling
in loose folds behind, which was described by a disgruntled
critic as utterly unnatural and consequently disagreeable. No
one living in the seventeenth century can ever have known a
natural shape.

The French evolved yet another method of holding out the
skirts called *les plis Watteau* after the artist who has so happily
recorded the loose sacque back, such as the lady wears who
turns her back to the viewer in his *Enseigne de Gersaint*. In Gay's
poem *The Hoop Petticoat* its shape was again supposed to be an
aid to a pregnant beauty, since its looseness would allow her
more easily to unlace, but the fashionable corset continued to
be so rigid that Horace Walpole says that a lady who
accidentally fell down was badly bruised by her 'Vulcanian
stays' and describes them as a 'steel bush down the middle and
a rail of the same metal across the breasts'.

Though the hooped skirt came back in the eighteenth
century it was never as extreme as the farthingale of the
previous century or the crinoline of the following one.
Madame de Pompadour's good taste and the elegance of the
period prevented such excesses, and portraits by Nattier,
Raoux, Fragonard and Boucher show the beauties of the day
with neat waists, rounded bosoms beautifully tricked out with

low, square *décolletages* and full, puffed sleeves ending in lace frills to set off the lower arm, one of the most seductive and feminine costumes of all time. In England Gainsborough's proud sitters, pictured against the woodland and rural backgrounds then fashionable, were tall and slender, in flowing satin dresses, fichued bodices and huge, feather-trimmed hats perched slantwise on white curls. In drawing-rooms on either side of the Channel an unusual shape appeared when both French and English ladies began to dress *à la turque*. Lady Mary Wortley Montagu was painted in Turkish robes obtained during her husband's brilliant sojourn as ambassador to the Porte; Maria, Countess of Coventry, was persuaded by Liotard to pose for him in robes he had brought back from the Near East; Rose Bertin made for Madame du Barry a dress in the Turkish manner in violet satin with lilac and white trimmings and a gauze turban; and *robes turques* formed one of the five categories into which Marie-Antoinette's wardrobe was divided when the Comtesse d'Ossun noted down all the *atours* of the Queen in her parchment book in 1782.

An equally unexpected influence came from across the Channel. The commercial treaty between France and England in 1786 resulted in Paris in a rage for the *style anglais*, and simple muslin toilettes such as those worn by Lady Betty Foster in Reynolds's portrait, or by Mrs Mark Currie when painted by Romney, replaced stiff satins and brocades. Rose Bertin was equal to any geographical change and created for Madame du Barry *une robe à l'anglaise* in white muslin, though she added ruches of Italian gauze. These comparatively simple toilettes with their pink or blue satin sashes and muslin frills agreed perfectly with Marie-Antoinette's idea of the rustic fashions required for life at the Petit Trianon; they represented a totally different approach to life as well as a different manner of dressing which, alas, was not to be developed. History caught up with fashion too quickly and the Revolution, like a clap of theatrical thunder which announces a transformation scene, caused the whole edifice of French elegance to vanish. When the storm was over the women were as nearly naked as they had been in ancient Greece. No change in the whole history of fashion was so abrupt and so total.

The Directoire and First Empire fashions demanded women with natural figures of good proportions which could dispense with artificial support. The Directoire corset was no more than a tiny, shaped belt which slightly constricted the rib-cage but left the buttocks free, but even this was scorned by the Three Graces of Paris, Mesdames Récamier, Hamelin, the wife of a rich army contractor, and Thérèse Cabarrus, later the wife of Tallien, sometimes called the Madonna of Thermidor, who was so lovely that she was compared to the Capotiline Venus. These ladies and Josephine Beauharnais, the mistress of the 'little General', preferred the vital statistics of their lovely bodies to speak for themselves. With their soft, unlined skirts falling from beneath the breast, and their flat shoes, their shape and way of moving was entirely different from that of their predecessors, corseted and encumbered with stiff skirts, panniers and heeled slippers.

In the 1830s the Romantic era ushered in a silhouette for the women strikingly different from the classic draperies of the early years of the century. Belts now pinched in the waist at its natural place and accentuated its smallness by enormous frills jutting out from off-shoulder *décolletages* supported by huge puffed sleeves. The maximum circumference of the figure was just above the elbow and just above the ankle. Skirts of only moderate width were neatly shaped into the waist and held out by starched petticoats, thus achieving a silhouette which, had Dior's habit of referring to lines by an alphabetical letter then been current, would have been called the 'X', since the tiny waist was equidistant from the wide hem and shoulders whose width led up to large-brimmed, high-crowned hats, figures so well portrayed by Achille Déveria in his series of drawings entitled *Les Heures de la Parisienne* of 1830. In the next decade the sleeves diminished, the skirts began to swell and once more the hoop returned to fashion. This new version, called a crinoline after the material used for stiffening, *crin* (horsehair) and *lin* (flax from which linen is made), was different from its predecessors and the bell shape which developed from it resembled neither the farthingale nor the hoops of the previous three centuries.

At first the skirts were only moderately full and held out by

starched petticoats stiffened with horsehair, but these were soon
replaced by a series of whalebone hoops attached by straps over
which a petticoat and then the dress were worn. The first
crinoline was woven by a manufacturer called Oudinet, the
creator of the stiff collar, who was thinking in terms of
neckwear, not skirts, but found his invention extended greatly
to his advantage. Crinolines were soon available in many
shapes and to choose the right one both for the wearer and the
dress was an important decision; some were round, others oval,
but all had a flattish front and were larger at the sides than at
the back, which gradually lengthened into the semblance of a
train. A new style of crinoline, first shown at the Great
Exhibition of 1851 and which quickly became popular, was
made of steel bands held together by tapes fastened by clasps so
that they could not be ripped apart, which the accompanying
advertisement proclaimed to be light, indestructible and full of
grace.

The revival of the hooped skirt is often attributed to
Charles Worth and its increasing girth to the pregnancy of the
Empress Eugénie, but both these assumptions are incorrect:
Worth did not become the Empress's couturier until 1860, four
years after the birth of the Prince Imperial and a decade later
than the reappearance of hooped skirts. Certainly there is no
doubt that Worth's creative ability and the Empress's vanity
combined to favour a style which offered full scope to that
'conspicuous consumption' later postulated by Veblen as one of
the mainsprings of fashion. The huge skirt gave the couturier a
large canvas for his designs and the Empress an unparalleled
opportunity of showing off her beauty in a sumptuous frame.
Once again, as in Marie-Antoinette's time, the actual dress
changed little, the tight-fitting bodice and wide skirt were a
background for the invention of a myriad surface decorations
such as Rose Bertin and Charles Worth loved to invent: but
neither of them created a shape, only variations on the
silhouette of their day. Eugénie was obsessed with clothes
and her vanity and super dress-sense is illustrated by many
anecdotes: she had her ball dresses made in duplicate so that
half-way through the evening she could change and reappear
fresh and dazzling. The Grand Duchess Elizabeth, sister of the

Czarina, had a similar habit, but when she disappeared at midnight to change it was into a different toilette enhanced by yet another parure of jewels.

When Eugénie accompanied the Emperor Napoleon III to the opening of the Suez Canal it was a splendid occasion for her to show off her lovely person and her magnificent toilettes, of which she took with her no fewer than 250. Princess Mathilde, who detested the woman her beloved cousin had married, said that all through her life Eugénie continued to be as mad about clothes as she was on her wedding day and described her as 'a trollop without temperament', to which the Empress replied by saying that Princess Mathilde, a talented amateur artist, was 'always dressed in her own water-colours'.

It is worth noting that during this era of extreme ostentation the three main courts of Europe, Britain, France and Austria, were presided over by young women, two of whom, Eugénie of France and Elizabeth of Austria, were not only great beauties but also fashion experts. Even the comparatively plain and simply dressed Victoria could not appear other than splendid and almost lovely in the lace-flounced satin dresses in which Winterhalter painted her, though hers were simple toilettes compared with the magnificent gowns of the French Empress surrounded by her ladies in the famous picture by the same artist. The romantic figures of these three empresses (for Victoria was soon to become an empress also) are the figure-heads of an epoch of pretentious display between the Romantic era and the world-weary *fin de siècle*.

Whether or not Worth was responsible for the crinoline, it is certain that he became heartily tired of it and longed to create something different, but no man's (not even an emperor's), or woman's, personal desires have ever been able to halt or hurry the pace of fashion. Napoleon III detested Eugénie's excessively wide crinolines and was said to have commissioned a farce which held this fashion up to ridicule. The leading lady appeared in a particularly grotesque example but the joke misfired, because the Empress Eugénie, hearing of this newer, bigger and therefore better crinoline, sent her maid to get its exact measurements so that she could have one made for herself on an equally large scale.

The wide skirts and off-shoulder *décolletages* demanded sloping shoulders which were considered a sign of beauty and good breeding, and the more closely a woman's shoulders resembled the top of a champagne bottle the more she was admired. Constantin Guys's drawings show a lively appreciation of this characteristic, but as the crinoline waned in popularity and sloping shoulders were no longer essential they seemed to disappear, and in 1878 Degas complained that one no longer saw them in society and considered this a deplorable sign of modern degeneracy.

The excess of tight-lacing, the immense size to which the crinoline had expanded, plus the weight of several petticoats, at last brought women to rebel. They were far from unanimous with regard to the scope of the liberty they longed for but it was clear that they wished to move about more comfortably. They began to consider their garments in the light of history and in 1847 Elizabeth Rigby, writer and traveller, who two years later married Sir Charles Eastlake, director of the National Gallery, wrote the first sensible account of dress which took into consideration its literary and historic role. This was a new approach, which was followed by the activities of the 'aesthetes' and the pre-Raphaelites, whose women members refused to be encased in a crinoline cage. Elizabeth Siddall was drawn by Rossetti with her long skirts hanging down limply, yet even this small step towards freedom caused the wearers to be accused of immodesty.

On both sides of the Atlantic groups began to form which encouraged women to abandon their hideous and uncomfortable clothes and return to a more normal shape. In America a campaign was launched by Amelia Bloomer, whose name became associated with the baggy trousers advocated by the reformers. Mrs Bloomer, who was not the originator of these garments but merely the agent who gave them wide publicity, edited a magazine for women in which she devoted some important articles to the peculiar, but comfortable, attire of a visiting friend. The response was tremendous and many women, Mrs Bloomer among them, adopted what became known as Rational Dress. Incongruously it added such feminine odds and ends as frills and bows to a mannish shirt-blouse or a tailored

1 Most civilizations show examples of body-painting, and John White's idea of a Pictish woman, drawn in the late sixteenth century after the artist-surveyor returned from the new colony of Virginia, was obviously influenced by the tattooed bodies of the Indians he had seen in the New World. British Museum, London.

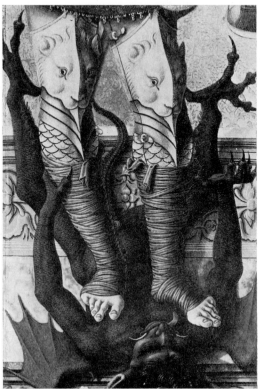

2 An example of body-painting of a truly surrealist fantasy is to be seen on the legs and knees of St Michael, painted by Carlo Crivelli in the fifteenth century. Detail from the Demidoff Altarpiece, now in the National Gallery, London.

3 Primitive man's worship of fertility resulted in many statuettes which show exaggeratedly corpulent limbs, but this figure, found in this century on the island of Gozo and tentatively dated the 3rd or 4th century B.C., is attired in a strangely modern flounced skirt. Valetta Museum, Malta.

4 – 5 The thin and the fat: two extremes of the female figure. On the left is Giacometti's 'Standing Woman', whose tenuous silhouette is even more wraith-like than that desired by the most exacting designer of unisexual clothes. Right, in strong contrast to Giacometti's skeleton statue is the sturdy figure by Jean Ipousteguy entitled 'Earth', which recalls all too clearly the massive fecundity of nature. Goth reproductions by courtesy of the Tate Gallery London.

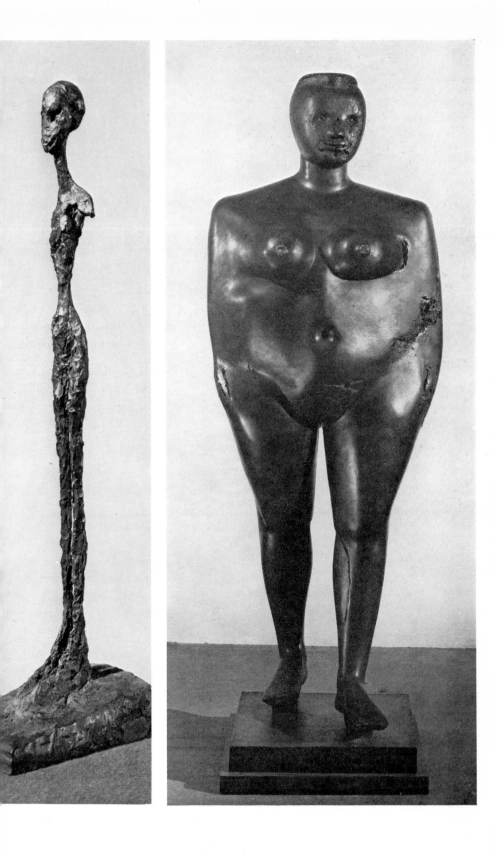

6 At the same time as the trouser suit increased in popularity there was a return to an exaggerated femininity. In the summer of 1968 Marc Bohan of Dior designed this be-frilled and sash-tied chiffon dress accompanied by a floppy flowered hat worn over shoulder-length curls. Drawing by Jeannette Collins, reproduced by courtesy of *The Times*.

7 Together with the revival of feminine fashions came an air of childlike innocence, and adults bravely donned dresses their teenage children could have worn. Philippe Venet suggested these two crêpe dresses in each of which a petticoat-bodice is teamed with skirts composed of flounces or tucks. Photograph by courtesy of Tissus Abraham et Cie.

8 Cardin's scarf-tied and neatly buttoned dark coat is pure schoolgirl, though the sophisticated black and white pattern of Courrège's belted model refutes the childish simplicity of its cut. Socks and comfortable strapped shoes complete outfits more suited to the kindergarten than to a morning's shopping at Harrods or Saks. Photograph by Patrick Hunt, reproduced by courtesy of the *Sunday Times*.

9 The rigid, long-bodied figure admired in the Elizabethan age is well illustrated in this portrait of Queen Elizabeth I in which her hip-length corset ends in a point on the stomach. An icon-like brilliance and elaboration is achieved by stiff sleeves, a jewelled ruff and head-dress, and long ropes of pearls attached on either side of the horizontal *décolletage*. By Federigo Zucchero, from the collection at Parham Park, Sussex.

10 A similar long-bodied effect was achieved by simpler means in 1962 by the Spanish designer Elio Bernhayer, who bared the neck and arms, dispensed with jewels but repeated the straight-across neckline and suggested the farthingale by stiffened flounces. Drawing by Bernhayer, reproduced by courtesy of the *Sunday Times*.

11 Far right, above. In the early seventeenth century an almost natural waistline and a soft *décolletage* composed such charming figures as this of the Duchess of Queensberry painted by C. Jervas. Here the famous beauty is seen with one of the aprons which Beau Nash would not allow his patrons to wear at the Assembly Rooms at Bath. National Portrait Gallery, London.

12 Before the First World War Paul Poiret was designing simple gowns like those above, with long unstiffened skirts falling to the ground which would not look amiss in the Seventies. Photograph Colomb-Gerard, Paris.

13 In the eighteenth century a rage for
Turkish fashions swept the salons of Paris
and London. Mme Rosalie Duthie was
painted by Etienne Aubry wearing a
version of oriental dress in which satin
trousers were worn beneath full skirts and
allied to a corseted bodice with puffed
sleeves, topped with a turban of doubtful
eastern origin. Reproduced by courtesy of
the Heim Galleries, London.

14 Dior's version of the trousered suit of 1968 was manly in style and accompanied by a severe shirt blouse and peaked Jules-et-Jim cap. Nothing feminine here, unisexual perhaps, but much that is coquettish and provocative. Photograph by Patrick Hunt, reproduced by courtesy of the *Sunday Times*.

15 Yves St-Laurent's knickerbockers recall Little Lord Fauntleroy but have not yet attained the success of that best-seller. Here, buckled beneath the knees and worn with buckled shoes, fitted hip-length jacket and frilled shirt held with a brooch, they suggest an androgynous rather than a girlish figure. Photograph by Patrick Hunt, reproduced by courtesy of the *Sunday Times*.

16 The slickly tailored suit of the late Forties, waisted, round-hipped and slim-skirted, was a style eminently suited to the talents of Digby Morton, whose London house was famous for the excellence of its cut. Here Nola Rose, one of the best-known models of the day, wears a grey striped model accompanied by a white blouse, white gloves and hat. Photograph by John French.

17 The over-feminine outfit of the Thirties with its plunge
neckline and horrible felt toque, a Matita model photographed by
Norman Parkinson in 1937, inspired Matita's present designer,
David Skinner, to create the neat suit (below) for the Cruise
collection of 1968. The eye-holes are enlarged and more clearly
spaced, the skirt and sleeves shorter, the smile and the hat
ignored. Reproduced by courtesy of Matita Ltd.

18 The Elizabethan beauty Mary
Cornwallis showed no trace of neck, for her
exaggeratedly wide and high ruff reached
up to her ears. The intricate embroideries
of her underskirt and huge puffed sleeves
with their Tudor roses veiled in finest
gauze compose a costume regal in its
grandeur. Manchester Art Gallery.
Photograph from Messrs M. Spink.

19 The lowest of low-cut bodices were de rigueur at the beginning of this century when the Italian artist Boldini painted this curvaceous lady, who was careful to follow a strict rule of the time – that no matter how much bosom was exposed it should appear to be a mono-bosom. The chic woman sometimes tucked a tiny gauze handkerchief or a flower into her corsage in order to disguise the offending cleavage. National Gallery, Dublin.

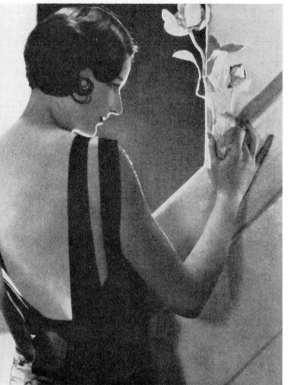

20 A quarter of a century later it was as essential to bare the back as it had been to expose the bosom earlier. A Patou-back meant no back at all, as this photograph of a Patou model of 1930 by the Baron DeMeyer proves. Reproduced by courtesy of *Harper's Bazaar*.

21 A fabulously overdressed lady of 1787
holds up her elaborately frilled skirt and
balances a huge hat laden with plumes on
her head while she buys a bouquet of
flowers from a street vendor crouched on
the ground. 'La Bouquetière' by Michel
Garnier, Archives Photographiques, Paris.

22 A more soberly attired English matron also wears a feather-trimmed hat but her panniered skirt is short enough to clear the ground. Her little daughter is dressed in a modified version of the same style, but her headgear is a ribbon-trimmed bonnet instead of a feathered hat, and the panniers are missing. 'The Cherry Seller' by Henry Walton, collection of the late Sir Osbert Sitwell, photograph Royal Academy.

23 By 1914 street wear had shed most of its *panache* though the lady buying a bunch of daffodils sports a striking stole and pillow muff of black and white fur. Head-fitting hats, ankle-high laced boots and the new handbag hanging on a handle were all noted by Joseph Edward Southall in Corporation Street, Birmingham, when he painted this picture a few months before the First World War broke out. Birmingham Art Gallery.

24 The bronze statue of Mrs William Van der Bilt, dated 1910, a work by Prince Paul Trubetzkoy, shows a restrained version of the slender pre-First World War women when the curvaceous opulence of the early years of the century was giving way to a straighter silhouette. Birmingham Art Gallery.

25 In 1967 Andrene Allen, then studying at the Birmingham College of Art, visualized this outfit as a possible garment for the year 2000. She conceived it moulded to the body with its lining bonded on to the fabric – no stitching any more. Already she has been proved not so far wrong. Reproduced by courtesy of the *Sunday Times*.

tunic and borrowed its chief item, the baggy trousers, from the least emancipated of their contemporary sisters, the Turks. A lithograph of the time shows Amelia Bloomer in full Turkish trousers gathered in at the ankles and a plain loose tunic which reached to the knees, a straw hat and parasol, which adds up to an attractive and certainly comfortable attire. Mrs Maria Jones, who wrote a book on Rational Dress, looks singularly unpleasing in a high-necked long-sleeved dress with a full skirt reaching to mid-calf, a pair of pants showing below. How such stuffily clothed figures can have appeared immodest is inconceivable, nevertheless the protests were numerous and women in Rational Dress were not permitted to enter a church. In 1970 an English judge reproved a witness for appearing in a trousered suit, but later in the year a special decree allowed them to be worn at Ascot.

A fashion authority of 1854 wrote with certainty that fashion was extremely aristocratic in its tendencies, that its every change emanated from the highest circles and that no new form of dress was ever successful which did not originate among the aristocracy. She asserted that, if the Bloomer costume had been introduced by a graceful scion of the nobility, it might have met with better success but that no American fashion could ever succeed in aristocratic England: it was beginning at the wrong end. Nevertheless Rational Dress was not totally lower-class; the Duchess of Montrose came out in plaid trousers and a short skirt well below her knees about which a spectator remarked: 'Her Grace will probably find some observations on her dress as well as her pursuits'. (She had just shot three stags.) When the Rational Dress Association met in London in 1883 Worth designed a costume for one of its members which consisted of knee-breeches with a short full skirt midway between waist and knee, and a blouse with frills at hem, neck and wrists. At another such meeting Oscar Wilde took the chair – the only man in the hall – and Lady Harberton made a sensation by appearing in black satin Turkish trousers, black velvet jacket, white satin top coat and *passementerie* sash, carrying a riding whip. The members of the Rational Dress Association believed that women would eventually wear trousers, though they envisaged these accompanied by skirts of varying length and fullness, which is not unlike the long-jacketed trouser suits of 1968 or the midi-length coat and trousers of 1970.

G. F. Watts was a declared enemy of corsets and a member of the Anti-Tight-Lacing Society, and among other fashion freethinkers in England were the wives of some of the *avant-garde* artists. Mrs Walter Crane and Mrs Alma Tadema both refused to wear the bustle and the over-trimmed clothes of the period, while Mrs William Morris and Ellen Terry insisted on 'practical dress topped by a graceful, circular cloak in winter, a loose scarf and a shady hat in summer'.

When the crinoline finally was ousted it was not by Rational Dress but by the irrational bustle, one of the strangest shapes ever adopted by European women when, with the aid of wired shapes and padding, they copied the protruding buttocks characteristic of the Hottentots whom white men in Africa were in the throes of exterminating.

The manufacturers were as enthusiastic over the new bustle supports as they had been over the crinoline and suggested innumerable different shapes composed of braided wire puffs of various sizes, some covered with stockinette and others of hair-filled hip-pads which were 'light, serviceable and infinitely chic'. Some, composed of black and white tempered wire which always regained its shape after pressure, must have been a priority requirement though, of course, at that time no lady leaned back in her chair or lounged on the sofa. At the same time manufacturers advertised bosom forms which could be stitched into the bodice and thus present the desired amount of bust to balance the immense outcrop on the buttocks.

Mrs Haweis, a well-known London writer on the 'art of beauty' and the 'art of dress', detested the bustle and refused to wear it, but neither did she like the 'aesthetic' style of dress affected by Mrs Walter Crane and Mrs Alma Tadema. She advocated the worst fashion heresy of all, i.e. to do exactly what one likes, and advised her readers never to pander to modistes, whom she considered tyrants, but behaved like a tyrant herself when she committed the signal unkindness of bringing out her seventeen-year-old daughter dressed in the clothes of her grandmother.

As the hated bustle deflated, a new and even more erotic

shape took its place. The polonaise had none of the panache of
the crinoline or the bustle's possibilities of concealment: it
presented the entire figure tightly encased from throat to knee,
where a flowing drapery descended to the floor and lengthened
into a train covered with frills which entirely hid the feet and
made movement almost impossible, so that only a figure of
perfect proportions and capable of gliding elegantly could
carry off such a garment successfully. It is noticeable that the
pannier and the polonaise, one hundred years apart, both came
at the end of two French dynasties and were replaced by
strikingly different styles, the one by the slender Directoire
muslin gowns, the other by the froufrou of Edwardian
petticoats.

The corset now devised yet another shape and drove a
ramrod down the front of the body so that the stomach
slanted inwards and the bust overhung the waist. The corset
was cut in such a way as to give maximum roundness to the
posterior. Extreme *décolletage* was essential for all fashionable
evening wear but no matter how low the cut it had to maintain
a 'mono-bosom', as showing two breasts was unthinkable.
This was the day of the 'professional beauties', referred to as
the 'stunners', among them Mrs Cornwallis West, Mrs Langtry
and Lady Lonsdale, whom crowds assembled to watch parade
or ride in Rotten Row, and whose magnificent figures adhered
to the then correct measurements of 38-18-38, a far cry from
the contemporary model size of 34-22-34 or Twiggy's 31-22-32.

The early years of this century are charmingly recorded in
the drawings of Charles Dana Gibson, who drew his healthy,
pretty young American women with their curvaceous figures
from life, for the three lovely Langhorne sisters were his
friends, one of them became his wife and another, Lady Astor,
the first woman to enter a British Parliament. On the stage
Camille Gifford became famous as the Gibson Girl, her bosom
moulded in black velvet standing out from her waist and
her waved coiffure projecting over her forehead.

Another new shape of the new century was the result of the
japonaiseries of the artists which brought the loose, kimono-
sleeved coat into fashion but grotesquely accompanied this
oriental style by western hats of immense size, flat as plates

and bearing aloft a forest of feathers or a medley of flowers.

Three men of such diverse personalities as William Morris, Oscar Wilde and Paul Poiret all fulminated against the fashions of their day, but the first two had little influence and few disciples, and only the last had sufficient authority to alter the prevailing modes. Poiret insisted on simple, unstiffened skirts falling from beneath the bosom to the ground and dispensed with all petticoats, which had such a disastrous effect on trade that the manufacturers of these garments approached the French Chamber of Commerce and a deputation was sent to the couturier to beg him not to eliminate petticoats from his models, but Poiret retaliated by introducing Turkish trousers and hobble skirts. Yet even he could not suppress the corset and the unconverted continued to support and mould their figures with whalebone and webbing. Nevertheless the female form became less curvaceous and remained non-committal until the 1920s when, as skirts gradually shortened and legs became more exposed, the bosom shrank in dismay, and by the middle of the decade a flattened non-bosom was as essential to the fashionable figure as a projecting super-bosom had been to an Edwardian beauty. A dress was a straight length of material, therefore the body had to be of the same shape and a well-known slimming course advertised 'tube figures for tube dresses'. Breasts, hips and buttocks were out, and the young men of the day had to make do with creatures singularly devoid of those erotic attractions sung by poets of the past.

The corset-makers had to alter radically the whole mechanism of their business; the actual materials of which corsets were made changed completely as satins, brocades, busks, bones and laces were discarded in favour of straight bands of elasticized material with unobtrusive suspenders to keep the corset-belt down and the stockings up.

This new non-support encircled the buttocks only, ignored the waist, and the separate brassière, descendant of the bust-improver, made its appearance, its task not to mould but to flatten any incipient roundness. Such a revolutionary change of silhouette had not been seen since the boned bodices of Louis XVI's court gave way to the miniscule corset of the Directoire. This was the opposite to that of the 1920s, for it compressed the diaphragm, emphasized the breasts but left the buttocks free, whereas the *garçonne* had a small elasticized band around her hips which left her waist and diaphragm unrestricted. It was assumed that she had no breasts.

Both the excesses of flat bosom and short skirt were modified during the 1930s, which saw the timid reappearance of the breast. The new bias cut, perfected by Madame Vionnet, rivalled the epoch of the Directoire in revealing women's figures in their entirety and demanded an equally high standard of good natural proportions, since it offered no tricks with which to conceal defects. Corsets were not possible beneath the clinging unlined dresses of *crêpe-de-Chine* or satin, for this new mode demanded a supple outline, not a rigid figure. Brassières were equally taboo because the backs of evening gowns were not only cut to the waistline but also back to the underarm. A Patou back meant no back at all and a new all-in-one corselette attempted the task of controlling unwanted curves. The ideal figure was that of Goujon's long slender nudes, yet half-way through the 1930s we have a striking instance of man's primeval love of the fat fertility figures reasserting itself, and Mae West with her hourglass shape became one of the great cinema stars. When she was about to make the film *Sapphire Sal* she cabled Schiaparelli asking her to make clothes for 'Sal' in the style of the 1890s, and sent the couturière a life-size nude figure of herself in the pose of the Venus de Milo.

Another anomaly of the 1930s was the combination of excessive masculinity with very feminine frills and in America the curious vogue of a black coat, an exact copy of a man's evening coat, white scarf and all, worn over a fluttering cut-on-the-cross silk dress and with a tiny flowered hat, repeated in terms of fashion something of the surrealists' approach to painting.

The padded shoulders were an immediate success and women gratefully accepted this easy method of improving their shape, and manufacturers appreciated the simplification it brought to the problems of sizing and fit.

Times of war and periods of political unrest usually bring about changes of style in dress, but in England during the

Second World War fashion was halted by rules and regulations set out by the Board of Trade, when sumptuary laws were obeyed for the first time in history. The amount of material permitted for each garment was strictly limited, each manufacturer was allowed to produce only so many styles each year and the public had to give up a number of clothing coupons in exchange for any purchase (seven for a dress, eighteen for a coat or suit) out of a total of about fifty. These so-called 'utility' clothes inevitably had a certain sameness of silhouette, but in France a totally different figure appeared. The shortages of material created variable shapes and the war-time Parisienne became one of the most extraordinary figures in the annals of fashion. Ankle boots with thick soles, short full skirts and broad-shouldered jackets were accompanied by hats as high and as extravagantly decorated as eighteenth-century head-dresses, the whole composing a curiously inharmonious and top-heavy silhouette as ugly as the circumstances which created it. These oddities were, of course, unknown to the English until after the war, when the first visitors to cross the Channel were as surprised by the French fashions as were the early travellers to France after the French Revolution.

The next complete change of silhouette was when Christian Dior presented his New Look in 1947. This was a conscious expression of a newly liberated world in which women could look like women and not like imitation soldiers, sailors or factory hands. The horror of war and the poverty of its aftermath were gradually fading, shortages of material were less acute and skirts could be fuller and longer, petticoats (suggested before the war) could swish in the newly discovered stiffened nylon, and small corsets (launched before the war) now cinched in the waist. It was expressive of femininity but, of course, it was not a New Look at all but a Last Look at a vanishing world. It was the afterglow of the sunset of French taste which had led the civilized world for over 400 years, the last coquettish womenly clothes before baby dolls, mods and minis took over. It was not destined to develop; a completely new expression of taste was to take its place and today the Olympic runner of 1,500 years ago with her short tunic resembles the modern girl more closely than the pretty post-war woman in her beautifully tailored suit of twenty-odd years ago.

Dior's later A-line of 1950 was an unsuccessful attempt to anchor the floating silhouette to a definite shape. It lasted less than a year but was significant in that it bypassed the waist. Once more the corset was out and only bosoms were in. The brassière became the most advertised item of clothing and the word 'cleavage' took its place in the esoteric language of fashion journalism.

The silhouette which replaced this over-emphasis on feminine development denied both waist and breast and concentrated on legs. The fashions became increasingly for the young and the yet younger girls who in their late teens sported clothes which a few years earlier would have been worn only by their schoolgirl sisters. Flat shoes, coloured socks, short skirts becoming shorter every season, coats and dresses were designed for teenagers, not adults. For the first time in history the couturiers ignored the woman and concentrated on the child. Courrèges's beautifully seamed dresses were nursery frocks translated into sophisticated terms; Philippe Venet's coats with turndown collars were similar to those that hang up in nursery-school cloakrooms.

2 Modesty

The recent fashion of transparent dresses, following on the total revelation of women's legs, has raised protests as violent, and as disregarded, as any other extremes of fashion in the past.

The concept of modesty comes and goes through the centuries rather as the cat came and went through the branches of the tree in *Alice in Wonderland,* each time reappearing in a different place, totally lacking in some periods but at others an essential ingredient of the current mode. Each time it selects a different part of the body as proper for exhibition or concealment, and what passes without comment in one country or period is considered indecent in another.

Modesty is sometimes suggested as the origin of clothes. This it most certainly is not; on the contrary, fashion has created modesty, which is a concept not found among primitive and unsophisticated societies.

One of the earliest and most universally worn pieces of adornment was the head-band seen on most primitive hunting peoples throughout the world, which in the course of time became the crown, or tiara, which symbolizes royalty and which has recently been revived. There is little doubt that early clothing was more concerned with rank or fertility than modesty. One of the first known garments was the apron of cowrie shells worn by a certain tribe of African women because in miniature the shell resembles the life-giving female organ. These shells were also buried with the owners to give them life in the other world, and until quite recent times were used as currency among several African tribes.

The first covering was almost certainly the skin of an animal, but it is unlikely that it was worn from motives of modesty: it may have been for warmth, but was more likely a status symbol. One explanation of the difference of dress between the sexes is that the best pelts were seized by the strongest men and that women had to be content with what was left over, and this practice, to which the egoism of the male subjected the female for some thousands of years, hardened her so well against the cold that she has been able to live in a state of semi-nudity ever since. It is certain that the male population of today could not survive an English winter with only one thin layer of nylon tights from foot to thigh, but the girls of 1968 appeared immune to such discomfort.

Legend tells us that when Adam and Eve were created they had a transparent covering, 'robes of light', of which the nails of the hands and feet are the only remnants, and that after the Fall when the disobedient couple plucked fig-leaves to put round them Eve wove hers into a wreath for her head and only Adam showed shame. So it is not remarkable that the young Eves of today are free from any similar hint of modesty.

In some primitive societies only the whores go clothed, thus bearing out Robert Burton's dictum in the *Anatomy of Melancholy* that the 'greatest provocation of lust comes from our apparel', and since nowadays garments are decreasing in number and size and the human body becomes more and more exposed, could it be that we are on the road to chastity?

The modesty which kept women hidden in capacious garments is based on the soundest of all theories of attraction: frustrated desire. The veiled woman of the Arab world, bundled up so closely that not so much as a nose could be glimpsed by anyone other than her husband and female servants, is, of course, the reverse of the houri. What cannot be seen can be imagined as celestially beautiful: such dreams might well be shattered by reality. The traveller Charles Doughty recounts an incident when a Muslim, with whom he had become intimate, as a great sign of friendship allowed him to see his wife unveiled, and sadly remarks that it is better for the 'moon of my delight' to be invisible than that the pock-marked face of a fat woman should be uncovered. Supposed modesty often masks a physical defect. A prejudiced observer related that Anne Boleyn wore a ruff at her wedding to hide a slight imperfection on her neck, and liked her hanging sleeves to be extra long to conceal the double tip of her little finger on the right hand.

The extreme modesty which forced the women of Islam to cover their faces has been relaxed in most countries; indeed the yashmak is now forbidden to Turkish women, who are forced to dress in European fashion, but in Persia, although the face-covering has been discarded, women still wear the chador, a long veil of coloured cotton which is draped over the head and falls to the ground, totally hiding the shape of the body but half allowing the face to be seen. This veil, of which Queen Farah strongly disapproves, is worn by surprisingly small girls and tots of six or so are already proficient in keeping it in place.

Those who discard decency throw away many weapons of attraction. There is a touching letter in Victor Hugo's reminiscences when he writes (in 1822) to his fiancée:

I wish that you feared less to have your skirts spattered with mud when you are out walking. Only yesterday I noticed with what care you took precautions, and I realize that your mother has asked you to do so, but it seems to me that modesty is more precious than a dress. . . . I cannot tell you, dear one, how I suffered yesterday and again today . . . on seeing passers-by turn their heads, and thinking that one whom I respect as I do God himself, should become before my very eyes the object of immodest glances. I wanted to warn you, my Adèle, but I did not dare to do so because I could not think of how to express myself. You mustn't be seriously alarmed but it needs so little for a woman to excite the attention of men. I implore you in future, my beloved Adèle, pay attention to what I say, unless you want me to strike the first insolent creature who dares to look at you. . . .

So great an emotion from so small a cause arouses dismay as well as astonishment in a world accustomed to bikinis and mini-skirts. Victor Hugo would have applauded the action of Virginie, the pure young heroine of Bernardin de St Pierre's romantic novel *Paul et Virginie* who, rather than strip to swim

ashore, preferred to be drowned. The romantic concept of
feminine purity endured throughout the nineteenth century and
the modesty of the heroine is a constant theme of the early
English novel.

Western fashions concealed the figure but revealed the face.
For hundreds of years women were shrouded in voluminous
robes, super-tunics, kirtles, wimples and coifs which hid their
figures, feet and hair; even their hands were rarely seen beneath
their long sleeves. A potent influence was the medieval fear of
the flesh for, strange contradiction in an oriental religion which
worshipped a woman both as a divine Virgin and as the
Mother of God, the medieval Christian Church taught that
women were snares sent by the Devil to seduce men and
encourage their fall, so the less seen of them the better.

The question of the display of the breast, now once again a
subject of interest, has been always hotly debated. In some ages
it has been accepted as natural; others have associated its
exposure with debauchery. Some thousands of years ago
Ishtar with her multiplicity of bare bosoms was a revered
goddess of fertility but in 1967 a small town in Austria was
torn with strife because after a long period of neglect a
seventeenth-century statue of the Virgin was restored by the
local council who wanted it to function as a fountain, as it had
originally done. The church authorities disagreed. They
maintained that the spouting breasts of the Virgin would be no
longer understood, and in defence of their point of view asked
the mayor how he would like to see a statue of his mother in a
public place with water pouring from her naked bosom.

The fashion for bare breasts came and went in the west. In
France a round bosom was greatly admired, and is clearly
exposed in Fouquet's twin paintings of Agnès Sorel, mistress of
Charles VII, one of which shows her wearing a plain muslin
coif and the other as the Virgin with a magnificent jewelled
crown on her head, but both show her bodice unlaced and
turned back to expose one lovely breast. Bared breasts became
known in the following century as *l'espoitrinément à la Venise*
because it was much favoured by the Venetian ladies, and
particularly by the courtesans who rouged their breasts as well
as their cheeks. A seventeenth-century traveller reports that

'the women wear gownes, leaving all the neck and the breast bare, and they are closed before with a lace, so open, as a man may see the linnen which they lap about their bodies, to make them seeme fat, the Italians most loving fat women. They show their naked necks and breasts, likewise their dugges, bound up and swelling with linnen, and all made white by art'.

The school of Fontainebleau has left charming pictures of the royal favourites in a state of semi-nudity. Diane de Poitiers is seen at her toilette choosing jewels from a box before her, a gauzy cape thrown back to expose her bosom. Gabrielle d'Estrées, whose *décolletages* were so low that the Pope threatened to excommunicate her, is seen sitting in a bath with her sister, both wearing their pearl drop earrings, with attention drawn to the breasts of one sister by the other pinching her nipple. Later, more prudish generations hid this picture which for many years was thought to be lost, but the original was found late in the last century concealed behind a curtain in the Préfecture de Police in Paris, and is now in the Louvre.

Such immodesty was not a feature of English fashions until the early seventeenth century, when the peculiar style of a ruffle worn close to the neck with the dress in front cut away to beneath the breasts was worn by unmarried women. 'Their breasts they embusk up on high, and their round roseate buds immodestly lay forth to show at their hands there is fruit to be hoped', wrote a disapproving observer. Inevitably the Church railed against the sin of pride and denounced 'naked breasts, necks and shoulders, flouting and fantastic habits' and a poet deplored 'those rising mounts, your displayed breasts, with what shamelesse art they wooe the shamefast passenger'.

The sophistication of the eighteenth century rejected any expression as blunt as nudity and required the titillation of suggestion rather than plain statements of fact. The beauties painted by Nattier allowed their bodices to slip off in order to reveal one breast but the taste of the later years of the century was for a more formal presentation. Madame la Pompadour appreciated all the etceteras of fashion and she was not painted in the nude, or semi-nude, like her predecessors in royal favour. The grandeur of the court of France, and the good taste of the age of Reynolds and Gainsborough in

England, ignored obvious ruses and sly hints and preferred a strict *tenue* in singular contrast to its morals.

It was left to the parvenue beauties of the Directoire to bring back the bosom to view, but by the time that Mesdames Récamier, Tallien and Hamelin appeared in their neo-classical robes modesty was as out of date as the monarchy. With their fine muslin gowns, which they sometimes damped so that they would cling more closely to their figures, they were more nearly naked than women had been since classical Greece. Madame Récamier was reputed to have launched the chemiseless fashion; *à la sauvage* was the name of a fancy dress composed of transparent gauze over flesh tights, and Madame Hamelin appeared at the opera *en amazone* in a robe which left her body uncovered from one breast to the opposite hip, and she walked bare-breasted in the Champs-Élysées. The fashions of the *Merveilleuses* resembled those of ancient Rome when Seneca complained that he saw 'silken clothes, if you can call them clothes at all, that in no degree afford protection either to the body or the modesty of the wearer, and clad in which no woman could honestly swear she is not naked'.

During the First Empire fashions were far more modest, for once in power Napoleon turned his back on the questionable characters of the *nouveau riche* smart world and insisted on more decorum at his court. He detested the semi-nude dresses and had all the fireplaces bricked up in the palace hoping that cold, if not modesty, would force the women to be more fully covered. The Empire dresses pushed up but did not entirely disclose the breasts but their roundness was considered as important as it had been in the days of Agnès Sorel, and false breasts of wax were worn, if nature had not been sufficiently obliging, with a film of gauzy material draped over them to hide the join between flesh and wax.

In the 1820s breasts were more modestly covered but their contours emphasized by cleverly cut bodices shaped and gored to give maximum roundness and to emphasize the 'cleavage', a word not used in this connection until the Second World War when once again this shape came into fashion.

During the many centuries when breasts were prominently featured they were often referred to as 'rounded globes'

and it was left to the mid twentieth century to present them as
torpedoes. This extraordinary fashion appeared in 1956 when
brassières were made with pointed tips so stiff that they almost
pierced the tight sweaters then worn. After the torpedo-points
were flattened, foam rubber was used to mould those bosoms
which were not the exact shape required and the trade began to
talk of 'tirage' and 'cantilevered comfort,' but advertised the
'no-bra' as the 'best bra'.

If the dresses with transparent tops first shown in the spring
of 1968 collections in Paris ever became popular, it would
spell the end of all brassières were it not that many women's
bosoms are unsuited to total exposure. Nevertheless the new
transparency certainly heralds a return to bosom display.
Several international clubs have been canvassing the possibility
of having their Bunny or otherwise named lady attendants
stripped to the waist, and the name of No Bra Bar has been
suggested for a night club.

A modest predecessor of today's see-through dresses were the
'peek-a-boo' blouses of the early years of this century. Made of
fine muslin or *broderie anglaise,* they revealed nothing more
startling than a solid cambric corset-bodice elaborately trimmed
with ribbon-threaded insertion, well shaped over the shoulders,
beneath which was not only a corset but also a batiste chemise
and/or a pair of combinations, yet they caused a furore and were
described as the depth of depravity. Mary Quant's play-clothes
of 1964 which showed sections of openwork between bust and
hips were the immediate precursors of the near-nude outfits of
Ungaro, whose brief bloomers, boleros and daisy-appliquéed
bare bosoms startled the Press of 1968. The development of
this trend towards nudity, which Eric Gill believed to be the
future of fashion, would be a triumph for central heating over
the English preference for discomfort and an example of
fashion carrying through a tendency to its logical conclusion.
It would be also one more example of the truth that what is
new is only something which has been forgotten – for an
Egyptian fresco shows Queen Nefertiti and her husband
Akhnaton wearing ground-length transparent gowns through
which their bodies clearly can be seen. Pausanius later described
Egyptian fabrics as 'woven air'.

Yet nineteenth-century academic art is full of the most striking nudes in the most unexpected positions: possibly one of the most erotic statues of all time is that of Eça de Queiróz, Portugal's great writer, in bronze frock coat and trousers, who stands in a Lisbon square clasping from behind an opulent nude female who is, of course, Fame. More usually a certain air of unreality was essential for the nude, or semi-nude, to be acceptable: Alma Tadema found he could paint naked women to his heart's content provided he included a Grecian column, a trireme at sea, or a sandalled slave to create an air of make-believe classicism. Nevertheless prejudices still exist today and only two decades ago a photograph of Marilyn Monroe in a state of nature was traced with difficulty and expensively suppressed when she became a star, as it was thought such a lavish display of her person would damage her box-office appeal. The beauties of today, although they reveal a good deal of their physical attributes in bikinis, are rarely sculptured in the nude. Elizabeth Taylor has not yet been put on exhibition in the round, yet at a time when the slightest exhibition of bosom or leg was considered shocking Cléo de Mérode exposed her extraordinary sway-back and projecting buttocks in an unforgettable pose sculptured by Falguière.

Even in these permissive days a nude statue of Field-Marshal Viscount Montgomery would cause quite a stir, but it was customary for Romans to have their heroes sculptured in the nude. Nearer to us in time Voltaire was represented in the nude by Pigalle, and Napoleon, sculptured by Canova, much more than life-size and totally nude, obstructs the hall in Apsley House. And what town councillor today would erect a statue similar to that of the Manneken-Pis in Brussels?

The recent revelation of women's nether limbs is the culmination of a prolonged strip-tease which has been going on since Rational Dress began to be discussed over a hundred years ago. One by one corset-bodice, camisole, combinations, drawers, petticoats and corsets have been discarded until the skirt itself is scarcely more than a hip-band.

The whole subject of underwear is of comparatively recent date and is really a history of the Emperor's Clothes: they do not exist. In ancient Greece the girls might wear a shift

beneath their short tunics but adult women's robes reached
the ankles and though occasionally 'a tunic, still unsewn, lays
bare her gleaming thigh' the breasts were not exposed as they
were in the earlier civilizations of Crete and Egypt.

The Spartan fashions shocked the Athenians, who could not
believe their girls virtuous, since they discarded their clothes to
race and wrestle with young men, but an appreciative spectator
likened the girls with their long golden manes and lithe limbs
to race-horses. The Roman woman was more modestly clothed
than her Greek counterpart and in early republican days a
woman out of doors scarcely revealed more of her body than
does a nun today.

During the Middle Ages a shift was the usual wear by day
and bare skin by night, the separate petticoat or kirtle not
making its appearance until the sixteenth century, when it was
more often a splendid underskirt revealed by the robe or
gown rather than the piece of lingerie which it has become.
Even the corset was often outer wear, not an undergarment,
and a boned bodice did duty for it. The first *caleçons*, or drawers,
recorded in western Europe were worn by Catherine de' Medici,
who insisted on riding side-saddle in order to show off her
well-shaped legs, and caused a scandal by wearing drawers.
Had a plain Englishwoman in her entourage followed the
Queen's fashion she would not have become a French duchess,
for in a hunting accident when she was flung off her horse her
magnificent limbs were clearly revealed, and the duke who
picked her up decided they more than made up for her plain
features. Nowadays no girl with a lovely body need keep such
a light under any bushel, and bikinis on the beach, thigh-high
skirts, see-through blouses all advertise what modesty once
would have hidden.

Drawers, like so many other luxuries, reached Europe from
the Orient and eventually came to England by way of Venice.
At first they were worn only by prostitutes, who often had them
made of gold or silver cloth, but drawers did not enter an
honest woman's wardrobe until the nineteenth century. An
inventory of a 1771 wardrobe which includes an immense
number of items does not even mention them; in any case, at
that time underwear was extremely scanty and usually consisted

of a chemise and one or more petticoats. In Europe drawers were considered a wholly masculine garment. Frenchmen opposed women wearing them, and the women in turn were shocked by Scotsmen wearing the kilt without them. Drawers did not finally become respectable items of female underwear until the ankle-length tubular drawers were worn under the immense crinolines which were apt to blow about in the wind or to shoot up in front when the wearer sat down. An embarrassing incident occurred at the Paris Opera when the great ballet dancer La Camargo insisted on the dresses being shortened and took the precautions necessary, but some of the *corps de ballet* did not, and the Paris police intervened and issued an order that all dancers in future must wear drawers.

The 'great day' of underwear was during the 1890s and the first two decades of this century. The long tube drawers of the 1840s and 1850s and the petticoats which covered the crinoline vanished when this contraption was discarded in favour of the bustle, and the combination was born, a shapeless lawn or cotton garment, with a modest *décolletage*, which reached below the knees, where it was finished off with lace-edged frills. With the *cancan* in the 1890s frilled drawers and flounced petticoats reached their ultimate elaboration and from then on a woman's trousseau laid emphasis on a dozen of everything, hand-made, hand-embroidered and edged with fine lace, particularly the petticoats because the necessity of holding up the trains of both day and evening dresses showed off the elaborate froufrous beneath.

Open-leg drawers and combinations of anything but erotic design continued to be worn, made of cambric or cosy wool, but the loose chemise went out of fashion by the end of the first decade of this century when it and shorter knickers fastened at the sides were teamed with long boned corsets. With the slim dresses of the First World War the great days of underwear were over and the 'teddy-bear', or all-in-one combination-and-drawers with the fastening inside the leg opening, replaced both chemise and drawers, and with the *garçonne* short-skirted dresses of the mid-1920s 'bloomers', or closed drawers, made their reappearance, all too often in unattractive silk stockinette.

The sexual ambivalence which has characterized women's costume during the last decade is far from being a novel feature in the history of dress. The wearers of the gaily coloured trouser-suits with their matching caps which added to the colour of the London streets during the cold winter of 1967 – 8 were related to the nineteenth-century 'emancipated' women, who in their turn could look back to trousered examples of the sixteenth and even twelfth centuries. These early trousered women were clad thus because when travelling or going to market on horse-back they rode astride like their husbands – more a case of convenience than a whim of fashion.

During the days of Elizabeth I the masculine attire favoured by women was noted with disapproval by Stubbes, who complained that the women wore 'doublettes and jerkins, as men have here, buttoned up the breast and made with wings, welts, and pinions on the shoulder pointes, as mannes apparell is for all the world'.

Nearly a hundred years later Pepys noted the ladies of honour walking in Whitehall dressed in riding garb 'with coats and doublets with deep skirts, just for all the world like mine, their doublets up, their breast buttoned up, wearing periwigs and hats'. It was not only in their riding dress that women aped men but frequently ordinary walking dress was a parody of the male costume though often enriched by feminine furbelows. 'Some pretty young ladies dressed like men in velvet coats, caps with ribands with laced bands, just like men'; others carried their laced hats beneath their arms and some went so far as to hang a light rapier at their girdle so that a poet wrote: 'Sir, or Madam, choose you whether You are one or both together'.

Most of the jackets borrowed by the ladies from their cavaliers had immense turned-back cuffs trimmed with three large buttons and a row of similar buttons down the front which were never fastened and, though critics twitted the women for this bisexual costume, the dashing coat with lace frills emerging from its wide cuffs and the flared tails of the coat held out by stiffened skirts created an extremely elegant figure. This, from 1780 to 1795 when for a brief moment English fashions were paramount in Paris, was called *le frac*,

but when women added large brimmed hats trimmed with
feathers and flowers it created a singularly androgynous effect.
Even Marie-Antoinette, most feminine of women, scandalized
the court by being painted in the uniform of the French
guards.

A different but also half-masculine half-feminine idiom was
adopted during the First Empire, when walking dresses showed
waist-short jackets with winged lapels buttoned high over the
breast which gave a very mannish air to a costume whose only
claim to the classical was a slender skirt and laced sandals.

Another more eccentric man-woman costume was devised by
those Parisian ladies in the mid nineteenth century who were
suggestively called *les lionnes*. This consisted of the surrealist
combination of a short crinoline, tailored coat, trousers and
jackboots, yet this curious mixture of skirts and trousers was to
reappear when dress reformers began their activities in 1860.
Hitherto all pseudo-mannish garments had concentrated on the
upper portion of the female anatomy, adding manly coats and
cocked hats to wide skirts; now the reformers ignored the
upper part of the body, concentrated on the lower and
concocted the unaesthetic union of trousers plus short skirt
which was revived in the winter of 1968 when feminine coats
were worn over trousered legs.

Although the dress reformers of the 1880s advocated
trousers, the militant suffragettes never did so, nor did the
boyish-girl of the 1920s, who considered these garments
suitable only for sport or on the beach, when flannel or linen
trousers were correct; occasionally very feminine 'cocktail-
pyjamas' were worn in country houses by the more advanced
younger set.

The wearing of actual male clothes was confined to a few
well-known exceptions. George Sand dressed like a man
during her liaison with Sandeau and then only when they
went to the pit of a theatre where women would not have
been welcomed, or to a little restaurant. The keeper of one,
Monsieur Pinson, used to say: 'When she's dressed as a man I
call her Madame, and when she dresses as a woman I call her
Monsieur.' Sarah Bernhardt, too, liked to wear suits and in
the evening was often seen in black velvet knee-breeches and

jacket very like a model shown in Saint-Laurent's autumn collection of 1967. In the 1890's knickerbockers were taken up as the smart wear for the new sport of cycling and the Prince de Sagan in knickerbockers, Norfolk jacket and straw hat led a contingent of similarly dressed friends, both male and female, to the rendezvous in the Bois de Boulogne which became known as '*l'allée des vélos*'. By the turn of the century bicycling was no longer fashionable and the 'bockers' gave way to short, i.e. ankle-length, skirts. Only Lady Harberton, tireless dress reformer, clung to her divided skirts and elegant breeches, but not even the most militant suffragette ever suggested wearing trousers.

The erotic combination of mannish *tenue* and feminine charm which added to the success of Vesta Tilley in the early years of this century was given a new and special character when Marlene Dietrich appeared in her white satin dinner suit with jewelled revers and a white top hat on her blonde curls, a recipe brought up to date by Twiggy in tails and topper. The trouser suits and white flannels which Marlene and her friends wore in private life, together with Garbo's more casual grey flannels and beret, helped to develop a very definite fashion which is still with us. Honor Blackman's black leather 'Avenger' suit of six years ago was a direct descendant of such histrionic gestures, but by the time her replacement, Diana Rigg, came out in a 'cat suit' these had descended from star-rating to suburban parties. Girls wearing trousers had become usual in the streets of London in 1966 but for some years young women in trousers were not accepted in business, and the edict banning women students at Oxford from wearing trousers on official occasions was not lifted until 1968, and then only after serious consultations had taken place between the Vice-Chancellor and the principals of all the women's colleges.

While the girls were busy making their nether limbs appear masculine, the boys retorted by growing their hair to lengths previously considered feminine, until it was a wise child who knew father from mother. Mademoiselle Maupin would not be noticed in her disguise today, which would no longer conceal her sex, and both she and the Chevalier (alias Chevalière) d'Eon would have found themselves quite at home in the streets of Chelsea in the 1960s. Indeed, the characteristic feminine silhouette of 1966 was a long pair of legs topped by a thigh-high cape, for the girls believed, rightly, that legs lie less than faces and left it to their nether limbs to proclaim their femininity.

3 Top-dressing

The mystical significance attributed to hair and its association
with strength and fertility undoubtedly arose from its magical
power to grow after death, and as hair has been always a
symbol of life, so has its cutting been a sign of renunciation.
The tremendous ceremony which attends the vows of a nun
was repeated grotesquely in Ireland during the 'Troubles' when
girls who fraternized with boys on the other side had their hair
cropped, and again after the Second World War in France
when suspected female collaborators had their heads shaved.
The ceremonies which attended the hair-cutting in the past
were not entirely dispensed with when short hair became
obligatory for young women in the 1920s when the high priest
of this holocaust, Antoine, a Pole, made a fortune in Paris. His
long salon was alarmingly furnished with mirrors set at every
angle so that the clients, used to having their hair 'done' in
separate cubicles, could for the first time see themselves, and be
seen by others, from every angle.

With this sacrifice of what had been considered one of
women's greatest attractions, the modern young woman
symbolically denied her necessity to attract the male by erotic
associations and declared she would meet him as an equal.
Hitherto women's hair was thought to have such strong
sensuous appeal that the Talmud insisted it was immodest for
married women to go outside the house without a head

covering, and the Christian Church ordered their female
worshippers to cover their hair in church so that no lustful
thoughts should be aroused in their male companions. So close
was the fancied connection between a fine head of hair and
uncontrollable wantonness that many artists have portrayed
Mary Magdalene with thick wavy hair right down to her feet.

Until recent times the last grown women to wear their hair
hanging loose were those of the twelfth century, and the last
queen to be shown on her effigy with her hair loose, though
covered with a kerchief, is Berengaria, Richard Coeur de
Lion's queen. The Norman ladies liked to display their hair in
long plaits sometimes interwoven with ribbons which ended in
bags or tassels, but after the thirteenth century it was the
custom for girls to put their hair up on marriage. Eleanor of
Castile, wife of Edward I, scandalized the English matrons by
wearing curls down her neck and further shocked them by
following the French royal fashion of receiving visitors in her
oriel at Caernarvon while her hair was dressed. The belief that
free-flowing hair was only for the very young persisted until
the early years of this century, when great importance was
accorded to the day when girls 'put up' their hair and became
young ladies, but with the shingle in the 1920s this custom
vanished. Nowadays flowing hair is no longer a certain attribute
of youth: it is often the mother who apes her teenage daughter
and lets down her hair, as once aspiring adolescents copied
their elegant mammas and tried to put up theirs. The
compromise of the late 1950s of hair half up and half down (the
beehive chignon plus shoulder-length locks) has its historical
prototype, and Habrocames' description of Anthea's coiffure
in A.D. 200 reads like a woman's magazine of 1960: 'part of her
tawny hair was tied on the crown of her head but most of it
was long and blowing in the breeze'. Another antique fashion,
the pony-tail which can be seen on many classical figures, was
also successfully revived in the 1950s, helped by Picasso's
ravishing portrait of Sylvette and by its adoption by the young
Brigitte Bardot.

The immensely important role which hair plays in fashion is
only equalled by the obsession caused by its absence.
Presumably on the same principle that an anti-hero is of more

vital interest than a conventionally heroic one, women
banished hair from their armoury of attractions for nearly two
hundred years. The first hint of its coming demotion was when
Eleanor of Aquitaine married Henry II and became the first,
but not the last, French queen to introduce a new fashion to
the English. She brought with her the becoming *barbette*, a
band of white linen passed under the chin which half hid the
hair and on top of which was placed a small round hat to
which Queen Eleanor liked to add a veil.

The *barbette* was followed by the more enveloping wimple
which shrouded the shoulders and throat, reached up to the
ears and was fastened on top of the head. This continued to be
worn by the old and conservative for nearly two centuries and
can still be seen in the dress of some religious orders. Fashion
ordained that it was as important to cover the ears as the hair,
but before both vanished beneath all-enveloping coifs hair
made a last appearance in plaits arranged in a square over the
ears, a coiffure which can be seen on Queen Philippa's tomb in
Westminster. Coils over the ears were revived in 1914 but in
circles, not squares, and worn by schoolgirls, not women, when
the uncomfortable plaits were referred to as 'snails'.

The methods invented to conceal hair were innumerable,
among them the most becoming was the *crespine,* a stiff coronet
of gold worn high on the forehead supported by cauls of gold
or silver which bulged out over the ears, often supplemented
with a snood which entirely enclosed the hair. But most of the
medieval head-dresses were strangely and fearfully made:
immense convoluted shapes of stiffened linen attached to
close-fitting caps and the ugly but well-named ramshorn,
which consisted of two huge side-ornaments supporting long
horns decorated with veils, were only two of many
monstrosities. The difficulty of including a crown in such
curious head-dresses is forcefully illustrated in the picture of
Isabella of Bavaria on her marriage to Charles VI, when her
head-dress consisted of two high forks on the top of which her
crown was precariously balanced. But she was only fourteen,
which may excuse the 'pompes and gorgiastetez' of her attire.
Other examples of fantastic head-gear were brought by Anne of
Bohemia to England when she married Richard II, and there

is no doubt that these two princesses from central Europe did
much to popularize the monstrous head-dresses which reflect
the medieval love of the fantastic and produced the nightmares
of Hieronymus Bosch and the grotesques of Dürer and Urs
Graf. The hennin, however, is attributed to the French Marie
de Clèves, though the word probably derives from the old verb
gehenner, meaning to trouble or incommode, and this it certainly
did, rising two feet or more off the head and, as the correct
angle at which it should be worn was 45 degrees from the
perpendicular, in order to anchor this edifice many women
adopted the frontlet, a loop of wire covered with material,
usually of black velvet, which pressed down on the forehead.
So huge were these head-dresses that it was found necessary to
enlarge doorways 'because the ladies wore horns wonderfully
high and large, having on each side, instead of pads, ears so
large that when they would pass through the door of a room,
it was necessary for them to turn aside and stoop'.

The medieval anti-hair cult was carried to such extremes that
not only the eyebrows were plucked but, in order to achieve
an effect of total baldness, so were the hairs of the forehead.
Beauty comparable to Pisanello's *Princess of Trebizond* was
required to carry off such a fashion successfully, but the
Princess's huge turban seems perfectly proportioned to her
delicate profile. Her head-dress is the first appearance of the
oriental turban in the west, descriptions of which were brought
back by crusading knights, and which reappeared at the end of
the eighteenth century and again in the early nineteenth.

Women's hair did not escape from its medieval prison until
the latter half of the sixteenth century. The last to hide the hair
completely was the gable head-dress made familiar by Holbein's
portraits of Anne of Cleves and Anne Boleyn, in which the
latter surely hid her real character as well as her hair.
Elizabeth I's portraits are strikingly unlike those of her ill-fated
mother and the curls and decorations of the Virgin Queen's
coiffures vied in importance with the elaboration of her dress.
Nothing now was too good for the once neglected hair: jewels
decorated the head, pearls and other precious stones were hung
on high frontages, and the French hood, a small rounded frame
trimmed with jewels worn far back on the head, exposed the

front hair often trimmed with two rows of jewels known as the upper and nether biliments. Mary Queen of Scots is credited with originating the becoming head-dress called by her name, its front curving down over the forehead but stiffened to stand away from the ears, the lines of this cap repeated in the wired-out lace-edged gauze of her cloak, so well recorded in her portrait by Mytens.

One of the chief beauties of Titian's and Tintoretto's women is the many and varied coiffures they adopt, their elaborately plaited hair often entwined with ropes of pearls. One traveller describing the Venetian scene of that time says of the women: 'their haire is commonly yellow, made so by the sunne and art, and they raise up their haire on the forehead in two knotted hornes and deck their heads and uncovered haire with flowers and silks, and with pearles, in great part counterfeit'.

From time immemorial blonde curly hair has been an attribute of goddesses, queens and courtesans. Aphrodite rises from the sea, her curls blowing round her, Mary Magdalene's wavy tresses reach her ankles, the finely curled hair of Neroccio de Landi's super-blondes, the winding ringlets of Simonetta Vespucci painted by Botticelli, the fairy princesses of legend, the film stars of yesterday – all have fair curly hair. Curls, however, can be as varied as women or wine, and no connoisseur of fashion would mistake a Tudor curl for a Stuart, though there are occasional resemblances and the small, flat curls which decorate the forehead and nape of Queen Henrietta Maria repeat those of the dancing girls in the Roman frescoes at Herculaneum then, of course, unknown. The same coiffure is worn by *la belle Stuart*, who refused King Charles until after she became Duchess of Lennox and Richmond, but Lely's portraits show the King's other mistresses with shoulder-length curls. A less attractive seventeenth-century curled coiffure was a bunch of curls held out over the ears by wires such as Henrietta Duchesse d'Orléans wears in the miniature by Samuel Cooper, a fashion which, most strangely, was adopted by Marlene Dietrich when she played the Empress Catherine of Russia. But the ultimate in east-west head fashions undoubtedly is the huge hat with long pointed sides worn by Largillière's plump *Belle Strasbourgeoise*.

Historians credit one of Louis XIV's mistresses, Marie-Angélique de Fontanges, with originating the coiffure called after her because one day, when out hunting with the King, her hair came down and she quickly piled it on top of her head and knotted it with a ribbon, but this careless and no doubt attractive hair-do seems singularly at variance with the formal Fontanges coiffure in which the front hair is arranged in curled horns decorated by bands of stiffened lace and ribbon standing up to half a yard above the head.

After a period of simplicity when in England the beautiful Duchess of Queensberry was painted by Jervas wearing a flat cap which hides her hair and ears, women's coiffures began to vary greatly and in the late eighteenth century, though vastly different in shape and execution, rivalled in size and fantasy the medieval head-dresses, the latter entirely ignoring hair and the new fashions stressing its importance by the addition of false curls and padding. Addison, editor of the *Spectator* in 1711, devoted an entire number to the subject of women's head-attire which, he said, 'within my own memory . . . [I] have known to rise and fall above 30 degrees . . . some ladies were once near seven feet high, then it became lower only to rise again some years later.' Fashions in those days of leisurely travel took some time to reach the provinces and the wife of a local squire who had passed the winter in London caused consternation in the village when she appeared in a little head-dress when the country ladies were still wearing large ones.

England developed a local style in which a mass of curls covered most women's heads in an apparently natural manner but were powdered to make them look artificial – which they were. Lady Elizabeth Foster and *The Parson's Daughter,* both painted by Reynolds, and Romney's Mrs Mark Currie all show a mop of *négligée* curls which must have been contrived with the utmost skill.

Women's coiffures continued to expand, to rise and become more and more elaborate and Marie-Antoinette's clever modiste, Rose Bertin, liked to concoct huge 'poufs' which commented on contemporary happenings: the success of Gluck's *Iphigénie en Aulide* was celebrated by a high coiffure decorated with black flowers, Diana's crescent and a veil half covering the hair; the King's decision to be inoculated against small-pox brought a coiffure *à l'inoculation* which showed a rising sun and a tree round which a serpent was coiled; and the wars were recalled by poufs *à la Boston, à la Philadelphie* and *à la Marlborough.*

These head-dresses were so large that the wearers either had to hold their heads out of the carriage window or sit on the floor, and Mary Darly's caricatures of the time, one of which shows the coiffeur standing on a ladder to dress his client's hair, are hardly more outrageous than the originals. Some of these complicated erections were only taken down and re-dressed very occasionally. One coiffeur, who asked his client how long it was since her head had been 'opened and repaired', was told it was above nine weeks, to which he replied he thought this was 'as long as a head could well go in summer . . . as it begins to be a little *hasardé*.'

Hats are late-comers on the fashion scene, are of rustic origin and originally were worn by men, not women – indeed Henry VIII actually issued a proclamation forbidding women to wear them. In the classical world the shallow hat with a pointed crown worn by some of the Tanagra figurines is its only example and was most probably more a shield from the sun than a fashionable accessory. European women only wore hats when travelling on horse-back and the earliest models were replicas of men's. Rubens painted himself and his first wife wearing almost identical head-gear and the Cavalier ladies and gentlemen both wore wide-brimmed, plumed hats, while their Puritan contemporaries did the same minus the feathers. The Spanish fashion of a tiny riding hat, seen to perfection in de Llano's portrait of the Infanta Isabella Claire Eugénie, of a small puffed velvet crown attached to a tiny brim over which curls a white feather, was also a steal from the men.

Hats were a recognizable sign of social class and in a portrait of a Tudor baby prince the status of the woman who holds him is made clear by her plain-brimmed, high-crowned felt hat: had she been the child's mother she would have worn a coif or jewelled head-dress. The flat straw hat was for centuries the sign of a country girl but became fashionable about the middle of the eighteenth century, and when

Gainsborough painted the elegant Mary Countess Howe in a brocade lace-trimmed gown and a plain flat hat it was a striking novelty. Some hats grew larger and larger; Betsy Sheridan, younger sister of Richard Brinsley, recounts that the diameter of her new hat was identical to that of her new tea-table, which her descendant, and present owner of the table, states is twenty-nine and a half inches.

In the late eighteenth century fashionable English picture hats replaced gauze and satin poufs. Marie-Antoinette's famous portrait by Vigée-Lebrun which shows her holding a rose in her left hand was repainted with the sitter in the same pose, but instead of the high pouf she wears a flat wide-brimmed straw hat tied with a ribbon. Madame Vigée-Lebrun painted Madame du Barry in a similar hat and two other *style anglais* hats are recorded in her accounts with Rose Bertin.

Post-Revolution coiffures went to the opposite extreme of the elaborate head-dresses worn at Marie-Antoinette's court, hats vanished and tiny 'spoon' bonnets covered the newly cropped heads. Thérèse Cabarrus, later Madame Tallien, emerged from prison with her curly dark hair in small wisps round her forehead and cheeks in what became known as the coiffure *à la Titus*, and in England Lady Caroline Lamb, with less reason, had her hair cut almost equally short. The lack of hair was an excellent excuse for the revival of the wig and Madame Tallien ordered no fewer than thirty in different shades from whitish-fair through ash-blonde to Titian red.

Soon women's hair grew longer and when Napoleon became Emperor and created Josephine his Empress something more elaborate was required, yet it was essential that it should not recall the coiffures of the past monarchy. The result was a classical bandeau and chignon framed by a small wired collar, known as a *cherusque,* which rose up behind the head and carried a faint memory of medieval courtly fashions, but owed nothing to the styles of the *ancien régime*.

The post-Empire style showed a complete contrast. Hair was parted in the centre and sleekly smoothed back into a coil on the neck in what was known as the 'Chinese' coiffure such as Madame Devancey wears in her portrait by Ingres, but towards the middle of the 1820s curls returned to fashion.

47

Coiffures once again became complicated, with high twists on top of the head and bunches of ringlets on either side. The so-called 'Apollo' knot was often encircled by jewels or flowers but for the morning plain pinchbeck circlets were worn called *malibrans* after the popular opera singer. Hats became of major importance; high-crowned, wide-brimmed and elaborately trimmed with huge bows and feathers, they flaunted through the 1830s until dispossessed by the modest bonnet.

Most of the mid nineteenth-century coiffures covered the ears but for a brief interlude they appeared with a plait looped round them such as Queen Victoria wore at the time of her wedding. As the Queen grew older the plaits disappeared but she clung to the centre parting and smoothly banded hair all her life, adding in her widowhood the pretty caps of pleated tulle which looked the acme of Balenciaga chic to a recent generation accustomed to undecorated but thinning pates of short hair. Among the Queen's subjects a state of simplicity did not last long and ringlets returned and were worn in a dozen different lengths and styles for a quarter of a century.

The Empress Eugénie often wore her hair in a large bunch of ringlets on the nape of her neck but varied this coiffure according to whether or not she was wearing a tiara. Many of her ladies liked to smooth the hair down on the sides of the face and then turn it into shoulder-length ringlets, variations of which coiffures can be seen in the well-known Winterhalter picture of the Empress and her ladies. When the Princess Alexandra married the Prince of Wales she wore her hair in long curls falling over her shoulders, but after her wedding put it up.

Eugénie's rival in beauty, Elizabeth, Empress of Austria, was so dominated by her fear of losing her beautiful hair that she spent hours every morning having it brushed by two maids, and every hair that fell out during this ceremony was carefully collected and presented to her on a silver salver. She insisted on Winterhalter painting her *en déshabille* so that her magnificent hair, which she usually wore in great loops round her head and neck, would be seen to reach her knees. At no other period was hair fetishism more noticeable: it was considered almost a virtue for a woman to be able to sit on her hair.

48

Dante Gabriel Rossetti was obsessed by women's hair and his pictures of Jane Burden, later William Morris's wife, with her immense mass of dark, strongly curled hair, and of the blondes, Alice Wildman and Fanny Cornforth, all display his fascination with the wealth and vibrant beauty of their exceptional hair.

On these heavy *chevelures* tiny toques replaced bonnets, often perched over the forehead with the back hair confined by a snood or *bavolet,* a ruche which swelled backwards and sideways out of the hat and hid the hair.

The 1870s saw the end of ringlets and hair was twisted into coils of extreme complication from the crown of the head to low on the nape until, as the century neared its close, the fashions once again became simpler with the return of the 'Apollo' knot and the craze for fringes. These soon became known by the name of the beautiful Princess of Wales, who favoured this fashion, and were worn by young and old, complemented by small toques which also became associated with Alexandra. A few of these were still tied under the chin, the last of a mode in head-gear which had lasted all through the nineteenth century.

Before women settled down to considering millinery a wholly feminine preserve, they borrowed two more styles from the men. One was the soft Homburg made fashionable by Edward VII and which, carried out in tweed, was worn by many newly emancipated women, and the other was the 'sailor'. This low-crowned, stiff straw sailor hat became the usual summer wear for both mistresses and maids and snapshots of the pre-1914 days show beaches, or country views, with the ladies all wearing 'sailors', which were also correct for cycling and tennis. 'Sailor' hats, kept on by elastics under the chin, became the chosen summer head-gear of innumerable girls' schools and did not vanish until the Second World War, when the austerity regulations caused school uniforms to be temporarily abandoned.

In 1890 a revolution in hairdressing took place when the great Marcel invented an entirely new method of curling the hair. Now, instead of the round ringlets which in one form or another had been in vogue for thousands of years, Marcel's

pointed tongs created rippling waves which clung to the
contour of the head. Curls and ringlets disappeared and waves
ruled every head; to be Marcel-waved was every woman's
ambition, only the aesthetes and the poor abstaining.

Inevitably this simple, potentially classic fashion became
elaborated, the size of the head was increased as the waved hair
was arranged over ever more monstrous hair-pads known as
'rats', huge chignons were held in place on top of the head by
tortoise-shell pins, and the back hair was kept in place with large
tortoise-shell slides. On top of these confections immense
plateaux of straw or velvet served up a mass of flowers or
feathers and were skewered on to coiffures with long hat-pins.
These huge hats were known as *matinée* hats and to matinées,
then very fashionable, ladies wore them though it was obvious
that anyone sitting behind them would not be able to see the
stage. Before the First World War it was unthinkable for any
woman, wealthy wife or working girl, to be seen in the
street without a hat. Smart women even wore them in their
houses, and Madame de Greffulhe is described entering her own
salon, usually preceded by two footmen, with one of her
enormous hats on her head.

An even more revolutionary invention than the Marcel wave
was the wonder machine first used in 1906 by Nessler, a
German hairdresser who patented his invention under the label
of the 'Nestlé' permanent wave which, when it came into
general use, offered the curls of a goddess to every girl with
five pounds to spare. Not every woman wanted to avail herself
of such a privilege. In 1918 women had obtained the right to
vote and many were determined to show their freedom in a
sensible way by throwing off the thraldom of uncomfortable
fashions. Already in 1912 a few young women had adopted the
Dutch cut, i.e. a straight fringe and straight shoulder-length
hair, and after the war the shingle of the 1920s became universal.
No Eton-cropped flapper of that decade would have believed
that hair-pins, false hair and wigs would ever return to fashion,
such extravagances recalled the days of women's subordination
and everyone was convinced that the bad old days would never
come again. The sight of young women in the streets with long
'bedroom' hair flowing unchecked would have been as shocking

in the 1920s as in the Middle Ages when women's hair had to be concealed in a coif.

Before the shingle became universal the hair was as carefully hidden as it had been during those far-away days but, instead of exposing the forehead, this was now entirely invisible, young ladies wore forehead ribbons and such vamps as Theda Bara and the young Gloria Swanson sported lamé turbans which barely allowed the eyebrows to be seen. Later the hair-bandeau became the hall-mark of the great tennis player Suzanne Lenglen, and the neat small heads of the 1920s were well hidden by beige cloche hats. The greatest modiste was still Caroline Reboux, who had known Worth and the Princess Metternich but had so well trained her assistants that they (or their descendants) could create a head-hugging cloche with the same assurance as the large pre-war hat, carefully cutting and pulling the felt into the right shape for each individual face – a hat then was as carefully fitted as a dress, not something just put on the head. Reboux died in 1927, aged 90, and was succeeded in her profession by a triumvirate of talented women, Agnès and two Roses, Rose Valois and Rose Descat, the latter a friend of Marie Laurencin who drew for her the charming picture which she used as her signature. Agnès, a sculptor by profession, became famous for her turbans which she draped with such expertise and which so well became her own handsome head. In the mid-1930s Madame Suzy knew better than anyone how to confect the small nonsenses which were worn not only by day but also by night. The fashion of the evening hat, launched in Paris during the first decade of the century, never penetrated to England, and when a smart London hostess in the 1930s, exquisitely dressed in a Parisian gown and Suzy hat to match, wished to take her dinner-guests on to the fashionable Four Hundred night-club she was refused permission to enter.

The cloche hat gradually shrank in size, or rather in depth, and tilted to one side to reveal a wind-blown curl on one cheek. Berets, also side-tilted, were much worn until hats made an abrupt change of position – they went to the back of the head and completely exposed the forehead, an item of negligible importance for the previous two decades.

Towards the end of the 1930s a strong wave of
anti-practical, pro-feminine fantasy swept into fashion, curls
and fringes reappeared and the coiffeurs exhorted their clients
to grow their hair and wear it piled on top of the head
trimmed with flowers and jewels as it had been a hundred years
earlier, but before this could become a popular style the war of
1939 turned everyone's eyes away from such follies to matters
of greater importance. The tiny dolls' hats launched by
Schiaparelli with such success vanished, though, as hats were
'unrationed' and no new styles evolved, the forward-tilting hat
with small crown and upturned brim continued to be worn
until the deplorable head-scarf made its appearance. At first this
was knotted on top of the head like a Negro mammy's, with a
roll of hair protruding on the forehead and another at the nape
of the neck, but soon, like any East European peasant's,
became tied under the chin, a horrible fashion which is still
with us today, more than quarter of a century since the
disaster which forced such poverty upon us.

The problem of how the women in the Forces should arrange
their hair occupied the attention of the Board of Trade, who in
1941 published a series of photographs showing what they
considered suitable styles for women in uniform. These were
of a surrealist impracticability which included such hard-to-
arrange coiffures as two or three tiers of sausage curls
protruding beneath military caps, page-boy bobs and immense
rolls on the forehead.

The French had followed a completely different path and
during the German occupation had concocted extraordinary
hats composed of any odds and ends of felt, material, feathers
and ribbons which came to hand. These grew larger and
larger until they almost rivalled in size the fantasies of the
Middle Ages and as bicycles were the only method of transport
the sight of the Parisiennes in short skirts and these monstrous
hats must have been quite extraordinary and caused more than
one post-war critic to query the much-praised French taste.
The Parisiennes retorted that they had made these outrageous
models to ensure that German women, who wished to copy
chic French fashions, should look even more ridiculous than
in their own dull clothes.

The revival of the hat proper was due to Dior, who with his New Look in 1947 showed the first real millinery to be seen for nearly a decade, but Balenciaga's tiny pill-box, varying slightly in shape, size and pose, was the great post-war success, and will always be associated with Jacqueline Kennedy, now Mrs Onassis.

During the 1950s a number of amazing coiffures were launched and, to achieve the bulk and height they required, another new method of curling hair was invented. Now it was wound round large rollers of plastic or horse-hair and when dry thoroughly back-combed, with the top hair brushed smoothly over the surface, when the whole edifice, about as solid as spun sugar, was sprayed with fine lacquer to hold it in place.

The milliners paid no attention to this development and continued to make head-hugging bonnets and hats like fur cosies, with the result that milliners and hairdressers went their own ways and the public went bare-headed. A generation grew up without a hat to speak of, and when in the winter of 1967 hats attempted a come-back they were wild-Western, brilliantly coloured cowboy felts, not 'ladies' hats.

Lanvin has persistently tried to revive the picture hat but had no real success until the summer of 1968, when her suggestion of large-brimmed hats heavy with roses was adopted by the English young, who looked adorably inconsequential in mini-skirts and maxi-hats worn over long straight hair. The separate race of milliner-modistes has more or less died out since the war and most couture houses have their own millinery salons and make their hats as complements to specific costumes, but in 1970 a faint revival of the hat was a noticeable fashion.

4 Singular supports

One of the greatest fashion changes which has come about during the last decade is in footwear. For the first time for nearly two centuries shoes of brilliant colour have enlivened our city streets and the strictly utilitarian role forced on our feet by the drab colours of nineteenth and early twentieth-century shoe styles has been discarded. Shoes are once more a source of pride and adornment.

Man, for ever torn asunder by the twofold significance he attaches to clothes, wishing at the same time to expose and hide that of which he is proud, often attempts to solve the problem by decorating the object in question which is thus both concealed and displayed. No part of his anatomy illustrates this procedure more clearly than his attitude to his feet and their covering.

The foot has always been a subject of fetishism and the shoe a protection in more than the physical sense. Its mystical power is expressed in many customs and legends: 'Over Edom will I cast out my shoe', said the Psalmist, meaning that he would annex that territory as a conquest; among Slav and Latin peoples as well as among the Germans a present to the bride from the bridegroom of a shoe was a sign that the girl considered herself his property; a memory of this practice lingers on in the custom of throwing a shoe after a newly married pair as a symbol of their lost liberty. To go shoeless was at one time a sign of mourning, and the wearing of one shoe only a portent of death or victory. King Pelias was warned against a man with one shoe, and Jason arrived to kill him so shod.

From remote antiquity men have worn simple flat-soled sandals made of leather whose correct preparation is the oldest craft known and antedates weaving. In times of famine starving people have chewed leather and, since such treatment obviously renders the skin soft and malleable, could the first preparation for footwear have originated in hunger? Because of the unpleasant odour of the skins, partly derived from the urine once used in the preparation, dyers and tanners were ostracized people; nevertheless Apollo was their tutelary deity and a statue of the god, Apollo Sandalarius, stood at the entrance to the street where sandals were sold in ancient Rome.

In the Christian calendar St Crispin was the shoemakers' tutelary saint and on his name-day a procession of the fraternity made its way through the city of London. Shoemakers can also claim among their company the distinguished philosopher Jakob Boehme, who was both cobbler and mystic.

The complex emotions with which humans have regarded the foot is illustrated in the story of Cinderella with its insistence on the mystique of the shoe. The story was first told in ancient Egypt when the heroine, called Rhodope, was bathing in the Nile and an eagle carried off one of her sandals which it dropped in the palace at Memphis. The king was astonished by its smallness, ordered a search to be made for its owner and vowed he would marry whomever the tiny shoe would fit. Rhodope was duly found and became queen, to the great envy and displeasure of the ladies of the court in whom Cinderella's Ugly Sisters clearly originated. Only much later did the sandal become a glass slipper and gradually other fairytale happenings were added, such as the mice, the pumpkin and the coach, but the theme remains the same: a small foot is worth a kingdom. So thought the Chinese and until this century followed the horrible practice of binding and deforming the feet of all well-born girl children in order to prove they were utterly helpless and therefore potential princesses. In China the smallness of a bride's foot was of great commercial value; her shoe was shown to the bridegroom's family and was one of the deciding factors of the bridal purchase price.

Feet remained taboo until recent historical times: when a special gift of stockings was sent to Marie-Anne of Austria on her marriage to Philip IV of Spain, they were refused by the envoy, who said: 'the Queen of Spain has no legs', meaning she would never allow them to be seen, but the poor little princess, aged 15, thought this meant her legs were to be cut off when she was married, and wept bitterly – an ingenuousness which made even her sad fiancé smile.

The earliest known shoes can be seen in Egyptian frescoes, where the wives and daughters of the Pharaohs are depicted wearing square-toed bright green, red or blue leather sandals, and shoes in these colours have been found in the ancient capital of Meroe.

The love of gay colours for footwear, now once more a part of contemporary fashion, is to be found among all early peoples. The Assyrians wore colourful sandals trimmed with jewels or fastened by jewelled buckles, and at the height of the Roman empire both men and women attached great importance to their brilliantly coloured and elaborately decorated sandals. Conservative citizens considered these unsuited to respectable women and thought they should be reserved for prostitutes, since their tunics were short enough to show their feet, an indelicacy proscribed to Roman wives. Even Roman soldiers were accused of paying more attention to their footwear than to their accoutrements.

The simple, flat-soled leather sandals were finished and tied in a dozen varied ways which denoted the status of the wearer, and a different number of straps were used for a monk or bishop. The intricate cross-lacing of the early Roman sandals is still seen today and Italy exports all over the world sandals remarkably similar to those worn when Rome was the centre of a vast empire. The upturned toe typical of the East with the thong between big and second toe is also still in current use, so is the backless shoe the Sumerians knew as mulu, which became the Italian *mula*, whence it passed to France and across the Channel as 'mule'.

The footwear of the ancient Britons was similar to that of

many other primitive peoples and raw cow-hide made the
pampooties and cuarans of both the Aran fishermen and
Scottish highlanders. The English climate obviously was not
suited to open-toed sandals and the Romans introduced
ankle-boots which became the usual wear in early Britain. Only
a hundred years ago a pair of Roman shoes was discovered in a
grave in Kent made of fine purple leather worked all over in an
elaborate pattern of hexagons, in shape remarkably similar to
the ankle-high wedge-shoe brought out by Perugia in 1938.

For five centuries after the Norman Conquest women's
skirts were so long that their feet rarely showed, although we
know the Carpenter's Wife in Chaucer's Miller's Tale wore
shoes laced high up on her legs (but are not told the colour) and
the Wife of Bath had scarlet hose and 'shoes full moist [soft?]
and new'.

Women's footwear continued to be relatively unimportant
until the reign of Elizabeth I, when the shorter-skirted
farthingale cleared the ground and revealed a pointed or
square-toed shoe usually made of silk or brocade often trimmed
with a cut-out decoration called 'pinking', which Dekker
mentions in his *Shoemakers' Holiday* as common to both men's
and women's shoes.

Women's feet remained quasi-invisible and though their shoes,
or pantofles, were of bright colours, sometimes embroidered
with gold and silver and worn with gaily coloured hose, the
idea of showing them caused one seventeenth-century French
husband to say he would rather see an English invasion than
his wife's feet exposed.

Had this jealous husband lived into the next century he
would have seen his wife's and other women's feet revealed by
the swing of their wide-hooped dresses. These shoes showed
sharply pointed toes with medium-height heels and high
vamps of leather or silk, the latter sometimes embroidered.
Stubbes said ladies' shoes were 'corked puisnets, pantoffles or
slippers of black velvet, white, green or yellow silk, with some
of Spanish leather embroidered with gold and silver'. Cork
shoes continued to be worn during the greater part of the
seventeenth century and were revived during the Second
World War.

The necessity of raising the feet above the filth of the streets, particularly when expensive and beautiful shoes were worn, was the origin of the utilitarian patten, once part of every woman's equipment. Mrs Gaskell describes the ladies of Cranford clattering home on their pattens, under the guidance of a lantern-bearer, about 9 o'clock after an evening party which included refreshments of an 'elegant economy'. As so often happens, what began as a necessity became transformed into a fashion. The fascination of extra height is part of make-believe all over the world: figures on stilts are found in many primitive rites, constitute one of the pleasures of every circus and are still seen in street carnivals. The special stilts made for brides in Persia and Syria were connected with the erotic desire of the husband to tie the beloved to him and prevent her running away and these raised platforms were often of great beauty, trimmed with gold ornaments and held on by gripping a jewelled toe-post between the big and second toes. In Syria curiously shaped pointed platforms of inlaid wood stood over a foot in height, but the Venetian 'chopines' outdid all others and a pair in the Museo Civico are no less than twenty inches high. Unlike the oriental platform-shoes which were accompanied by ankle trousers and bare feet, the Venetian chopines were hidden by extra-long skirts, and when a lady wearing them went out she appeared like a giant in comparison with the attendants who were obliged to support her on either side. Beneath this long skirt the nether limbs were clad in silk knee-breeches, stockings and shoes tied round the ankles. A traveller of 1605 recounts that the ladies seem a foot taller than the men 'because they walk on high leather-covered blocks of wood'. These high-soled shoes were designed to protect the wearer's dress from dirt but were also thought to safeguard virtue, for how could a woman run to a secret rendezvous in such cumbersome affairs? It was believed that the flat-heeled shoes which superseded the high clogs brought a change in morals as well as in costume. The extraordinary fashion of chopines lasted until 1670 in Italy but in most western countries it was known chiefly in the form of the lowly rural clog.

High heels always have been connected with erotic appeal

and considered one of the prostitutes' trademarks. Rarely have puritans had more reason to decry them than during the mid 1950s, when the new stiletto heels wrought untold destruction to carpets, parquet floors, the decks of liners and the floors of aircraft. Airlines called special meetings to discuss what could be done to make floors more resistant to the attack of spikes driven through the floors by the several stone weight of heavy matrons balanced on a pinpoint of steel. If women walked across a lawn they drilled holes and the damage done to carpets throughout the world does not bear contemplation. It was a new discovery in the field of metallurgy that made possible this device which, when first seen at Dior's opening in 1952, caused a tremendous sensation and stiletto heels became the rage. A gilding of the lily was to have the pinpoint of the heel set into a tiny ball of brilliants so that the wearer seemed to walk on air supported by a mere glitter of light.

Strangely enough this device was relatively comfortable if the shoe was well balanced, but cheap copies soon made it vulgar and in the course of a few years it vanished, to give place to the clobber heels fashionable in the late 1960s. In the meantime museums and houses open to the public were obliged to insist that visitors either should remove their shoes or wear overshoes, but this was only after a good deal of initial damage had been done, and the nuisance reached such a pitch that institutions provided rubber tips which could be slipped over the offending points, or large felt slippers which could be tied over the entire shoe. Private houses had no such rules and floors will show the marks of this fashion as long as they endure, while the damage to valuable rugs was so great that in some instances their owners took them up and put them away until the craze mercifully passed. This was by no means the first time that fashionable heels caused damage and in 1607 a pessimist wrote: 'You shall see tomorrow, The hall floor peck'd and dinted like a millstone, Made with their high shoes' but does not tell of what material the offending heels were made. At that period most heels were of wood or cork covered with fabric or kid, until the introduction of the layered leather heel called 'cuban' which became fashionable for walking shoes in the 1920s. The high heels worn by both men and women during the reign of George I curved under the foot in what looks a very unbalanced way, and the shape sponsored by Louis XIV and still called by his name was worn by both sexes until the French Revolution drastically altered fashion.

The curved Louis heel did not recover from its descent to the flat Empire slipper for several decades, and when it returned at the end of the century it was clearly understood that the greater the height the lower the morality: high heels were and are a sign of the prostitute.

Colour was as potent as shape and height in the erotic attraction of heels. Louis XIV's love of scarlet heels set a fashion which was followed by his courtiers and by the whole world, but it was blue heels which particularly offended one censorious magistrate in London. Isaac Bickerstaff asserted that the display in the window of a shoemaker in St James' would create irregular thoughts and desires in the youth of this realm and declared that, 'the said shop-keeper is required to take in these eyesores, or show cause the next court-day why he continues to expose the same; he is required to be prepared particularly to answer to the slippers with green lace and blue heels'.

This eighteenth-century misogynist would have approved of the quieter colours of the next century but he died when ladies still tied up their coloured shoes with ribbons of green, red or blue and adorned them with buckles.

Like so many other accessories, buckles had begun as purely utilitarian necessities for attaching the shoe firmly to the foot. In this practical role they were known in the fourteenth century but by the eighteenth they had become merely an adornment which was considered important to the shoes of both sexes. The ladies' hooped skirts were sufficiently short to reveal the foot and ankle and buckled shoes were as much a necessity for a serving-maid as for her mistress, the difference being only in cost.

How changed was the picture after the Revolution when Directoire fashions revived the classical sandal! The artist David liked his models to wear *cothurnes* tied with ribbons over naked feet, and Gérard painted Madame Tallyrand wearing such flimsy supports. The would-be antique but wholly delightful

dresses of the first decade of the nineteenth century were
accompanied by heelless slippers of coloured satin whose toes
were often square. Later tiny heels were added, very low and
placed well beneath the instep. These satin or kid *escarpins*, often
trimmed with flowers or lace and usually tied with ribbons,
were clearly visible during the whole of the 1820s when the
full skirts stopped short well above the ankle but, with the
advent of the crinoline, skirts grew longer until only the toe of
the slipper was visible. An alternative to the flat slipper was the
ankle-boot or low-heeled *bottines*, called *bottes polonaises,* of which
a clear view was given when the Empress Eugénie and her
ladies visited Biarritz and wore their crinolines sufficiently far
off the ground to show their neat ankle-boots. The Empress
never wore a pair of shoes twice but for once her extravagance
benefited others; her feet were so small (Cinderella again) that
her shoes were sent to a school attended by poor children who
learned to dance in an Empress's shoes. Shoe fetishism is a
well-known trait among fashionable women and Sarah
Bernhardt took no fewer than 250 pairs with her when she
went on a tour in America.

Though in theory the Victorian crinoline hid the foot, in
practice it was often revealed by the sway and swing of the full
skirt and feet were far more fully concealed when the bustle
and polonaise became fashionable, for with trains and skirts
touching the ground women moved as if on invisible rollers,
since no hint of their feet could be glimpsed. Towards the end
of the century the shaped but unstiffened skirts permitted the
wearer to raise them and display frilled petticoats and elaborate
stockings of a novel kind never before seen but which strongly
resembled the patterns with which the inhabitants of the
Marquesas Islands tattooed their legs. Uniformly black in
colour, these stockings were riotous with embroidered flowers,
butterflies, hearts, love-knots and sometimes enriched by the
insertion of real lace, but with them the choice of shoes was
limited. Most had pointed toes and moderately high Louis
heels, usually with one strap, and were of black or bronze
kid or black patent, but to adorn them buckles came back to
fashion. Stockings were known to the early Egyptians and one
of the earliest known foot coverings is a divided toe-sock found

in an Egyptian tomb, somewhat similar to the Japanese *tabi*, a white sock with a separate toe still worn with traditional Japanese costume. That stockings were important and costly items is illustrated by one of the carvings on the immense staircase at Persepolis which shows the neighbouring kings bearing tribute from their conquered countries to the great Darius, where a group of Parthians are depicted carrying trousers and a pair of stockings which clearly show the feet. In medieval times stockings, or cloth hose as they were then called, were worn by both men and women, but some were so important and expensive that in the sixteenth century they were considered gifts fit for a king. The first silk stockings in English history are said to be those brought by Sir Thomas Gresham as a present from the Spanish court to Edward VI. The first knitted stockings on record were given by her silk-woman, Mrs Montague, to Elizabeth I, which the queen found so comfortable that she said she would never again wear cloth. The French assert that the first knitted stockings came from the village of Tricot, near Beauvais, which gave its name to knitted garments.

The first stocking-frame in England is credited with a novelettish origin: in the 1590s a certain William Lee, Master of Arts and Fellow of St John's College, Cambridge, was courting a girl who refused him. She earned her livelihood by knitting and, in revenge, he invented a devilish machine which would deprive her of her livelihood but endeavoured in vain to persuade stocking manufacturers to use his new invention. His stocking machine was forbidden by law in 1598 and Lee removed to Rouen, where the court patronized his invention, but the murder of Henry IV and the subsequent internal troubles in France delayed his plans, and it is said he died in Paris of a broken heart.

At the end of the eighteenth century light colours were fashionable for women's stockings and embroidery often enriched those intended for full dress. The Empress Josephine had all her stockings embroidered with her initials, most of them in blue, her favourite colour, but she also had thirty-two pairs of rose-coloured ones. White was the fashionable colour during most of the nineteenth century and dark stockings did not become popular until the 1890s.

The first thirty years of this century saw little change in footwear. Toes and heels varied in height and width, but lace-up shoes and buttoned boots were either black or tan. Women wore white shoes in the summer and for tennis, sturdy brown boots for golf, 'co-respondents' (a court shoe with a tan base lace-patterned on white) with cuban heels for resort wear, satin or brocade court or strap shoes for evening. Fashions in shoes changed so slowly that if a good 'last' was made, new shoes in different materials could be ordered over and over again from the same shoemaker for several years. There was little effort to achieve any accepted international sizing in ready-made shoes and America must be thanked for the revolution which took place in this field. Every woman who wears a double AA fitting owes a debt of gratitude to I. Miller who, just before the Second World War, first imported into England the four widths of the A's.

The short skirts of the 1920s should have brought with them an increased awareness of women's feet. The fact that they did not is proved by every snapshot of that decade and the sad strap shoes bear silent witness to the relief with which those who did not have perfect legs and take a size 4 in shoes welcomed longer skirts in 1929. At first skirts were short in front and long behind but soon they were long all the way round, and shoes continued to be dull but were less in evidence. Towards the latter part of the 1930s an effort was made to shorten skirts for informal evening wear. Schiaparelli launched her 'ballet-length' dinner gowns with coloured 'tango' slippers tied with ribbons up the legs *à la* Vernon Castle (or *à la* Madame Tallien). Peep-toe shoes made their appearance and had a certain success but were considered rather vulgar.

The war put an end to such frivolities as coloured shoes, and the coupon scheme which required five coupons (later seven) for a pair of shoes out of a total of between forty and fifty per annum allotted to each person, plus the shortage of leather, made shoes one of the rarest items in the shrunken wartime wardrobe. In France immensely high 'platform' soles of cork replaced the unobtainable leather and gave to the short-skirted Parisiennes a strange swaying walk. Cork has remained in use for beach shoes for which the Italians have made some outstanding designs. Perugia's leather-covered cork-soled shoe was one of the most popular pre-war novelties, surprisingly and beautifully recorded for posterity in a painting by Pierre Roy.

The immediate post-war period continued to suffer from a great shortage of leather and shoes to be conservative in colour though they changed greatly in shape, but as skirts grew ever shorter more and more attention was paid to the feet.

Before the last war stockings were either of wool, cotton (which masqueraded under the name of 'lisle-thread') or silk with clocks on the sides and remained the 'flesh' colour first launched in the 1920s. The miracle fibre of nylon appeared in America during the war but was not known to the impoverished Europeans until some time afterwards, when the picture changed and in 1963 stockings had so much news value that English manufacturers were able to attract fashion journalists to a breakfast party to show them the new pointed heels and to instruct them in the mysteries of deniers and gauges. The 60-gauge did not arrive until 1951, the seamless stocking appearing the following year, but the semblance of total nudity of the legs was not popular until the late 1950s.

The increasing fashion for sandals and the display of bare feet has brought many hidden sorrows to light and few Europeans, their feet mangled from their childhood by badly fitting shoes, can walk barefoot with ease and pride. Oriental women, to whom shoes are unknown and who care for and paint their feet just as they do their hands and face, have feet of a natural beauty that is rarely seen on European beaches. Gérard de Nerval in his *Voyage en Orient* says that the women's feet with 'henna-painted toe-nails and anklets as exuberant as bracelets have a degree of seduction not found in western society where the grace and charm of that portion of a woman is too often sacrificed to the glory of the shoemakers.'

Early in this century such idealists as Isadora Duncan, Ruth St Denis and Martha Graham did their best to inculcate a love of and care for the naked foot, but the conditions of urban Western life demand protection and, except for the Flower Children, who in the summer of 1967 walked about dirty city pavements in their bare feet, people continue to be shod.

The obvious alternative to nakedness is ostentation and the footwear of the following winter was an example of total contrast. Feet were of an unexampled splendour and gold and silver boots worthy of Mercury plodded through the London rain. Colour once again played an important role and the previous summer's gaily coloured shoes were succeeded by boots as varied as the red, blue, yellow and green shoes that the Normans wore when they invaded Britain. Some boots were resolutely zipped, others had fancy lacings reminiscent of a more leisurely period, some were thigh-high in the style of an old-time pantomime boy, or Queen Christina as portrayed by Greta Garbo.

For the revolution which has turned footwear from objects of use into objects of beauty Italy is greatly responsible. Italian shoes brought not only colour but also comfort to women's feet and Ferragamo's unblocked leather shoes of undeniable chic are as soft and easy to wear as a pair of gloves. Both Ferragamo and Perugia were world-famous names long before 1939 and much of the post-war brilliance of colour originated in Florence where a lively memory of its fifteenth-century splendour is still potent.

The contribution made by Paris to the shoe market is in keeping with the French tradition of catering for a high quality market, and when Roger Vivier began to design for Dior he produced shoes which Madame Pompadour would have been proud to wear, lace-covered, bead-embroidered and £50 a pair. Behind these glamorous examples of the shoemaker's art lay a real feeling for shape and the shoes which have come from the Parisian Charles Jourdain have no equal in design and their influence is world-wide.

A totally new substance, named Corfam, made profound changes in the world of shoe fashions. It not only kept out the wet but allowed the feet to breathe, permitted a variety of bright colours and its construction eliminated much labour. Mary Quant was invited to style this new material, with the result that hordes of gay red, green and yellow boots enlivened the dull winter streets of 1967–8.

The stretch tights which became universal female wear in the late 1960s were first brought out by Morley, but their

'Gadabouts' of 1961 were rather thick, in a limited range of colours, and made little impact except on sportswear. It was not until 1967 when the mini-skirt made tights essential that lacy patterns and pretty colours appeared, and though they could not compare with those worn by the Renaissance pages they were extremely decorative. The only modern invention which outshines the splendour of fifteenth-century male attire is Lurex thread, which has given the girls of today shining legs of gold or silver which the men of the past would have not only appreciated but adopted.

Mary Quant designed for this new fashion also and hundreds of girls in the winter of 1967 – 8 shimmered from their ankles up to their thighs in her glittering tights which Cinderella's prince might well have envied, though her daisy-patterned tights were an even greater success.

In 1968 stockings became one of the high fashion notes of every outfit: fancy patterns of every weave and colour in wool and nylon appeared either as stockings or as full-length tights, footballer stockings for casual wear, knee-high socks trimmed with lace for sheer fun and metallic hose for glamour. Some of the best-known designers, notably Valentino of Rome, applied their talents to this new-old field and stockings could cost many pounds a pair. Clocks reappeared up the sides, in shining Lurex rather than sedate silk; whorls, dots, flowers and trails of ivy climbing up the leg made plain flesh-coloured stockings appear as old-fashioned as black ones did to the flappers of the 1920s.

26 Two contrasting aspects of modesty. Above: a late nineteenth-century lady imparting to her women friends the happy news that she is about to have a baby – words which could not be spoken out loud even to a couple of intimates. 'Le Secret' by Marchal. Photograph by Roger Viollet, Paris.

Beneath: a scene in a bath-house from a fifteenth-century manuscript which shows both sexes feasting and bathing entirely nude except for their hats and jewels. Bibliothèque Nationale, Paris.

27 Twiggy, the new star model who rose to fame in 1967, made no bones about being masculine when she wished to, and when dressed in tails and topper resembled the 'knuts' of London town so successfully portrayed by the music-hall singer Vesta Tilley before the First World War. Photograph by Justin de Villeneuve, reproduced by courtesy of *Queen* magazine.

28 The cult of the hermaphrodite in the early seventeenth century produced this amorphous figure which, like most mongrels, appears to combine the worst traits of both sponsors: a hideous female coiffure, a ruff common to both sexes, a masculine jacket puffed out with false bosoms, padded breeches held by coquettish bows beneath which appear stockinged male legs. British Museum.

29 A far more attractive but equally inconsequent combination of masculine and feminine traits was produced by Cardin's white satin hipster pants which reveal the navel, accompanied by a long black lace coat and, final incongruous touch, a baby's bonnet tied with a bow under the chin. Photograph by John French, reproduced by courtesy of the *Sunday Times*.

30 A novel feminine silhouette was proposed by Lanvin in 1967, when a flared cape similar to those worn by French schoolboys before the war revealed only a pair of legs, clad in dark stockings and shod in flat shoes. A beret also recalled the boys of long ago but the effect, helped by a chin-hiding fur collar, contrived to be incontrovertibly feminine.

Jeanne Lanvin

31 A sixteenth-century 'Scène Galant' shows the lady revealing what was then known as 'l'éspoitrinément à la Venise', from the habit of the Venetian ladies of revealing, and painting, their bosoms. Picture by Paris Bordone from the collection of Earl Spencer.

33 In 1967 Yves St-Laurent startled the press of the world by presenting models which had transparent bodices. One of the most noted of this debatable fashion was a navy dinner suit composed of Bermuda-length shorts, tailored jacket and dark blue chiffon blouse which intermittently revealed the model's breasts. Photograph by courtesy of Yves St-Laurent.

32 A far more outright bosom display was that of the Irish beauty, thought to be the second wife of the artist Robert Fagan, who painted himself and his spouse in the first years of the nineteenth century when she was wearing a dress which left the breasts entirely naked. Reproduced by permission of Mr and Mrs John Hunt.

34 Far more successful was St-Laurent's Hamlet-like black velvet *ensemble* of 1967, in which long black tights were allied to a black velvet jerkin, gold belted, and a floor-length, fur-edged velvet robe. If few actually wore this costume it certainly presaged the maxi-coat worn over a mini-skirt two years later. Photograph by Patrick Hunt, reproduced by courtesy of the *Sunday Times*.

35 At the end of the Fifties when women were paying more attention to their coiffures than their hats Lanvin-Castillo made an effort to win them back to millinery by producing a series of remarkably beautiful models which seemed to the uninitiated absolutely unwearable. Nevertheless a few beauties appeared in them and made the public think again about the attraction of headgear. Photograph courtesy of Debenham and Freebody.

36 Top right: To the delight of posterity a late eighteenth-century version of the picture hat was recorded by Madame Vigée-Lebrun in her charming portrait of the Russian princess Elizabeth Stroganoff wearing a wide-brimmed model trimmed with a ribbon and a large bunch of violets. Collection Prince Paul of Jugoslavia.

37 Bottom right: A 1966 English attempt to woo women back to hat-wearing was Peter Shepherd's feather-light but huge cloche of folded white organdie dotted with sprays of lilies of the valley, shown by the now-extinct firm of Woollands, Knightsbridge. Photograph by Van Pariser of the Geoffrey Sawyer Studios.

38 – 9 The small cap which hid all the hair (left) shown by Dior in 1960 was remarkably similar to the severe coif painted by Memling in the fifteenth century, but the wearers are strikingly different. The modern girl with her accentuated eyebrows, outlined eyes and smiling, painted lips in a sophisticated black dress is a far cry from the plain Flemish girl with her plucked brows, pale, unsmiling lips and discontented stare. Hans Memling, reproduced by courtesy of Messrs Wildenstein.

40 The early Twenties saw an almost total eclipse of the forehead and hair, heads were encased in turbans of dubious oriental origin and a smart Parisian was painted by Kees van Dongen wearing a topless, short-skirted lamé dress with a turban to match.

41 The Fifties version of an eastern fashion shows top model Shirley Worthington in a tiny black toque to which a large osprey appears to be attached by a jewelled brooch. With hair brushed back, ears and forehead uncovered, eyebrows accentuated and mouth, not eyelids, darkened, Shirley epitomizes the fast-vanishing ladylike fashions of the post-war period. Hat by Otto Lucas, photograph by John French.

42 The late nineteenth century and the pre-Raphaelite painters in particular were obsessed with the idea of hair and many of their portraits of women, especially those by Dante Gabriel Rossetti, gave great prominence to the vigour and luxuriance of the model's hair. Annie Miller (left) was one of Rossetti's favourite models and he painted her in 1860 with her fair curly hair streaming down on to her shoulders. From the collection of L. S. Lowry. Photograph by courtesy of Messrs Agnew.

43 The mid twentieth century gave hair an equal prominence but achieved magnificent coiffures without the help of nature, and new nylon fibres, many times finer than real hair, were used to create any type of colour required. A silver wig falling straight as water was designed to accompany a knitted silver dress by Belleville et Cie in 1967. Photograph by David Anthony.

44 The amazing versatility of Twiggy's features made her into a typical late Twenties flapper when Leonard restyled her short hair into the waves of a shingle, and draped round her shoulders that essential accessory of the period, a fox fur. Photograph by Barry Lategan, reproduced by courtesy of *The Times*.

45 The Baroness de Meyer, *née* Olga Cacciolo, wife of the famous photographer and a god-daughter of Edward VII, was one of the great beauties of her day. Sargent painted her early in this century wearing a large hat whose sweeping brim is laden with birds and veils. Birmingham Art Gallery.

46 The magnificent *panache* of the ostrich-trimmed hat was the subject of one of Gustave Klimt's most successful portraits, in which the broad plateau of the hat is supported by huge cushions of hair. Reproduced by courtesy of Marlborough Fine Art Ltd., London.

47 The girl of the late Sixties discarded all the extravaganzas of hair and hat which her grandmother affected and looked more to the moon than to feathers and flowers for her millinery. In 1967 Simone Mirman designed these nail-headed space-helmets, typical of their time and social climate. Photograph Associated Press.

48 The wide-brimmed hat had a lowly and rustic origin and was originally worn only by country girls. In the eighteenth century John Jackson painted the gardener's daughter wearing one of the wide straw hats then usual in rural areas, and also a pair of wooden sabots such as continued to be worn by European peasantry well into this century. Leeds Art Gallery.

49 A fifteenth-century French manuscript clearly shows the courtiers' feet shod in long pointed shoes which make the pointed toes of the late Fifties positively restrained. Bibliothèque Nationale, Paris.

50 Allen Jones recorded the Fifties' obsession with high heels and pointed toes in a series of hallucinating canvases such as 'T-riffic'. Reproduced by courtesy of Arthur Tooth and Sons Ltd.

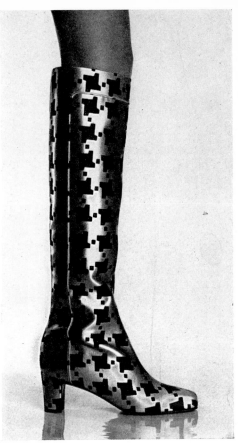

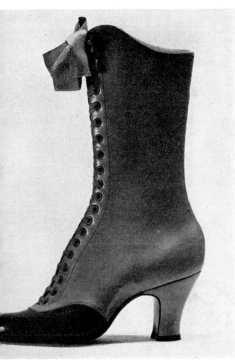

51 The revival of the boot in the late
Sixties did not mean repetition of previous
styles but a totally new look in which a
pleasing effect was more important than
protection. Dior's shoe designer Roger
Vivier chose Ascher's black and white
checkered satin for this knee-high boot.
Reproduced by courtesy of Ascher Ltd.

52 – 4 The famous shoe firm of Bally has at
their headquarters at Schoenenwerd in
Switzerland a fabulous collection of shoes
of all periods, including a number of
miniature shoes composed of enamel and
precious stones. Among more recent
examples are the three on the left. (Top) a 1902
boot of Nouveau Art inspiration, (centre) a
buttoned and buckled shoe of 1874,
(bottom) a 1915 laced-up boot which has
many contemporary equivalents.
Photographs by courtesy of Messrs Bally.

55 The revival of patterned stockings in the Sixties began by moderately classical designs such as those by Wolsey (above left) but the idea that woollen stockings could be chic was in itself a revolutionary one. However, it soon became accepted as high-fashion and in 1968 Lanvin suggested (below left) these fancy stockings and footwear as part of her novel bloomer dress. Photographs by courtesy of Messrs Wolsey and Jeanne Lanvin.

56 The so-called tango fashion, which included shoes tied with criss-cross ribbons up to the knees, was immortalized in a drawing in 1919 for *Harper's Bazaar* by Erté, the Russian artist turned Parisian who was famous for his sumptuous stage settings. Photograph by courtesy of the Grosvenor Galleries, London.

5 Fabrics

The present century has seen a new element enter the fashion
world: synthetic fabrics. Any wardrobe today, rich or poor,
consists of as many, if not more, garments composed of
man-made fibres as of the historic foursome of linen and cotton,
both derived from a plant, wool from an animal's fleece and
silk from the silk-worm. Now nylon, Ban-lon, Terylene,
Dacron, Crimplene, Corfam, and a host of other names as
non-natural as the materials they represent, by-products of
unpronounceable chemical formulas, have ousted the 'natural'
fibres which until today composed the only coverings known to
man. In the last decade children in Midland towns where these
miracle fibres are spun began to sing, when playing hopscotch
in the streets,

> Silk, cotton, rayon, nylon,
> Terylene, entylene, nicotine, pylon . . .

instead of their old cry of 'silk, satin, cotton, rags'.

Attempts to create artificial fibres were made early in this
century but for a long time the 'artificial silk' produced
was so horrible in appearance and so difficult to handle that it
was used mainly for cheap curtains, and in the fashion world
clothes made in it were considered vulgar.

Many of the fantastic names of the early artificial textiles
have been forgotten: who now remembers Nucolaine, the
Tricolette of 1919, the Rufflette of 1910, or Courtauld's

unfortunately termed 'Courgette'? Nor has the more
aristocratic 'Treebark' stood the test of time, though this
crinkled silk and Cellophane 'glass' material, both used
brilliantly by Schiaparelli in the 1930s, are the ancestors of the
uncrushable drip-dry and see-through fabrics of today. New
names are legion and recently one paper published a glossary
which included no fewer than twenty-nine different groups of
artificial fabrics of which many had several variants and finishes.
Among the most familiar are viscose, the first wood-pulp
derivative to be made in Britain, and Terylene, developed in this
country by I.C.I., originally discovered by John Whinfield at the
research works of the Calico Printers' Association in 1941. This
was declared a secret by the wartime Ministry of Supply but its
formula was sold to America for much-needed dollars and
therefore Dacron, as it was called in the United States, had
several years' start on its English parent. It was not until the
1950s that I.C.I., who had absorbed the Calico Printers, began
to study the market seriously with a view to launching Terylene
in the fashion world, but at first the material was too stiff and
difficult to sew for the intricacies of women's clothes and it
was with men's trousers that Terylene made its first big
success.

Nylon is the most versatile of all man-made fibres and there
are now some forty different types, including a 9-denier yarn five
times finer than human hair, which first appeared in 1939 but
owing to the war did not enter the stocking market in England
until later. The glittering Lurex which was also perfected in
America during the war did not reach Europe until the late
1940s.

Among the great successes of the last few years are Acrilan;
Ban-lon, popular for its soft handle and bulk without weight,
which has been strikingly styled by Ken Scott whose vivid
floral patterns were seen all over the world in 1967 – 8;
Calpreta, guaranteed by the Calico Printers to be non-
shrinkable; Dorlinic, a linen-type material remarkably crease-
resistant which is exclusive to Dorville; and Helanca, a Swiss
product whose stretch qualities make it eminently suitable for
socks and the new market for women's tights.

The turning point in the development of artificial fabrics

came during the Second World War, when all materials were
in short supply and the manufacturers and scientists used all
their ingenuity to find replacements for wool and silk in a
world where 'fashion' reached vanishing point but in which
humans still had to be clothed. The miracles produced in
France startled the European and American buyers and
journalists who straggled back in 1946 to see the first Paris
post-war collections. Some of these synthetic fabrics were so
lovely and their potentialities so exciting that many designers
realized not only that *ersatz* fabrics were possible replacements
for the classic materials but that certain new effects could be
obtained only with their aid. When the stiffened full skirts
which delighted a public accustomed to the skimpy silhouette
imposed by shortages of material were first launched by Dior
in 1947, it was not known what material permitted these light
dresses to hold their line, or of what the myriad frilled
petticoats were composed. It was some time before the secret
of the stiffened nylon was out. At first it could not be
bought in retail shops but was exclusive to the couture houses,
but when it became generally available an avalanche of feather-
light petticoats floated into the shops and in the late 1950s they
were sold for as many shillings as the pounds they cost when
first produced. Much of Dior's successful cutting and free-
standing shapes owed their crispness to the development of
these stiff but gossamer-weight linings.

The earliest recorded woven material is the fine linen made
by the ancient Egyptians, and from time immemorial the Nile
valley was the scene of the culture of flax and of a thriving
export business which continues today. So fine was the
material (in the past spun by men, not women) that it was
often transparent and from this soft clinging stuff were made
the ankle-length, straight dresses so often seen in carvings and
frescoes. The first patterned materials known were those of
the Minoan court ladies, some of whose dresses show wavy
patterns on a cream ground and a reticulated border on the
double apron which curves over the front and back, but of
what fabric they were composed is not known for certain
though it was most probably linen.

In Europe wool was the most important material. It made

the Greek chiton, the Roman toga and the early Britons' trousers and tunics. The art of making woollen cloth was brought to great perfection by the Anglo-Saxons and English woollens were held in high regard on the Continent, a prestige they have never lost. Edward I formed a guild of Merchant Tailors and Linen Armourers to protect and develop the industry, an edict confirmed by Edward III. For a time the importation of foreign cloth was forbidden in order to prevent undue competition and when this rule was relaxed the local weavers reacted violently against the foreign merchants.

A vigorous home market was developed by business men who catered for an expanding middle class, welcomed new inventions and continued to encourage the settlement of immigrant weavers. In 1546 the arrival of a 'new drapery' known as 'Bays and Says', a finer cloth than had ever been seen before and which was due to the skills of clever aliens, was celebrated in the doggerel: 'Hops, Reformation, Bays and Beer Came into England all in a year.'

The superiority of English woollen cloths continued up to this century, when the wool industry found itself menaced by the appearance of artificial fibres. The present International Wool Secretariat owes its being to a small group of Australian, New Zealand and South African woollen merchants who met in Melbourne in 1937 and formed what was then called an International Wool Publicity and Research Secretariat, whose London office consisted of three members and a staff of three. Although situated in three far-apart countries, the leading woollen producers knew that between them they supplied over 50 per cent of the world's wool, and realized that a combined effort was necessary to uphold the prestige of wool in the face of increasing competition from man-made fibres. Their early attempts to force wool into the high-fashion market were sadly unsuccessful, for they followed the lines then taken by most English firms who wanted to launch new merchandise: they either paid a Paris couture house to make a model from one of their materials or hired a French designer, but all too often it was only the name they acquired from which, like some religious relic, a sort of miracle was expected. In the 1920s a serious study of fashion in relation to mass-production was almost unknown in England and as no careful market research preceded these ventures, and as both manufacturer and designer were unfamiliar with each other's problems and methods, the joint ventures were nearly always failures and responsible for a hard core of resentment among those English firms who had experimented with foreign stylists.

A second, and more successful, effort to promote wool for formal wear was made in the 1930s but Schiaparelli's suggestion of tweed for evening was ignored, and it was not until after the Second World War when a change of social habits brought about a drastic change in fashion that wool was accepted for evening wear.

The present International Wool Secretariat follows quite different methods. It now has offices in twenty-one countries and its 'Woolmark' is legally protected in 101 countries. It has its technical centre in a building worth £1¼ million in Ilkley in Yorkshire, its fashion office in Paris and its menswear office in London; it publishes a fortnightly World Wool Digest and a quarterly Wool Science Review and uses the Press, TV and radio to make known its progress. It links its consumer advertising with merchandise available in stores so that end-products are featured together with brand-names and information on what they cost and where they can be bought – a far cry from the one and only high-fashion model with no past or future of forty years ago. The now famous 'Woolmark' has resulted in a large increase in the wearing of acknowledged woollen clothing of a high standard, but little of it is for underwear and its success in outerwear would have puzzled and displeased Dr Gustave Jäger, professor of zoology at the University of Stuttgart in the latter half of the last century. He believed in FIZICAL HELTH THRU DRESS and maintained that animal fibres must be worn next to the skin in order to control both the pleasant and 'noxious' emanations of the body. His Sanitary Woollen System of Dress sounds anything but hygienic to a generation accustomed to daily bathing and weekly laundering, for he insisted that a woollen shirt could be worn for at least six weeks before it needed washing. His name is perpetuated in the fashion-conscious London firm of Jaeger.

Linen weaving was another old-established industry in

England, though it never became a successful export, as
continental flax growers always appeared able to undersell the
British product. It was a necessity for any wardrobe of quality
for centuries before cotton was known, and linen composed the
wimples, bands, collars and ruffs which formed so important a
part of both men's and women's clothing from the thirteenth
to the eighteenth centuries.

Flax was known in antiquity and was grown and woven all
over Europe but became particularly an Irish industry which
produced the finest damask and linens, and its thread was also
used for Irish lace-making. Its tendency to crease has limited its
appeal as a fabric for dresses but a mixture of linen with
synthetic thread has led to improvements in this field.

In Europe cotton was a late-comer. It was grown and spun
in India at least as early as 500 B.C. and was also known in
Egypt in the pre-Christian era. The Arabs brought it to Europe
and grew it in southern Spain, where it still grows wild, and in
the thirteenth century some was exported from Barcelona.
Italy had early learned its use and the knowledge spread to the
towns of the Netherlands, whence Protestant refugees brought
it to England in the late sixteenth century. By A.D. 1600
cotton-weaving had begun in England, when the raw cotton
was imported from Turkey and Smyrna and called cotton-wool
because of the mass of fluffy white fibres which burst out of the
boll. This had to be woven on a linen warp and the fortune of
the Fugger merchant family was founded on the successful
weaving together of these two fibres which then composed a
popular cloth called 'barchent'.

The early seventeenth century saw the extraordinary
adventures of the East India Company, which first ventured
into the seas of the Far East in 1601, and brought back to
England fine 'cotton yerne' from the Coromandel Coast and
'callicoes light coloured, none of them course and sad cullers'
from Calicut (Calcutta) and delicate muslins from Mosul.

At the beginning of the eighteenth century Defoe was
writing of the 'fansie of people' for the East Indian goods
and noted that chintzes and painted calicoes, previously only
used for furnishings, now were popular for clothes, in
spite of an Act which forbade the introduction of Indian

silks and printed calicoes, either for clothing or furnishing;
like most other sumptuary laws, this was not effective.

Columbus, of course, had already seen the inhabitants of
Hispaniola dressed in fine and comfortable cottons but these
were not imported into Europe from the West Indies until the
end of the eighteenth century, when some ladies from Santo
Domingo arrived at Bordeaux in fine muslin gowns which
helped to develop a new fashion in Paris.

Cottons first reached France direct from the east when
cotton goods from the Coromandel Coast were shown in the
Foire de St-Germain in 1658, half a century later than in
England. These were considerably cheaper than the materials
woven in Europe and also very attractive – Madame de Sévigné
bought some for her daughter – and merchants soon realized
that the Indian cottons were damaging the French textile
trade. In 1736 an edict was passed which imposed a heavy
fine on anyone wearing garments of Indian fabric, and it was
not until 1759, over a hundred years after its introduction
into France, that the manufacture of *toile* was made legal.
Even then it was strongly opposed by the weavers of both
silks and woollens, who saw in it a dangerous rival to
their products.

After the East India Company's monopoly of trade with
India had ceased in 1813 the West Indies began to supply a
great deal of raw cotton. In the following century the
development of vast cotton plantations in the southern states of
America completely altered the conditions of the cotton market.
Manchester became the nucleus of what is now the largest
textile centre in the world.

Although references to silk can be found in records of the
fourth century B.C. the culture of the silkworm was not
introduced into Europe until the sixth century A.D. and silk was
not produced in any quantity until the eighth. Before then all
silk came from China and was brought overland by the Silk
Road which crossed the Central Asian plains and found its way
via Constantinople and Venice to western Europe, by which
time it was extremely expensive, and in the third century A.D.
one pound of silk was worth one pound in gold. The Romans
despised it and, considering its thinness and transparency

indelicate, continued to wear wool. Silk, like most other luxuries, was at first the prerogative of royalty and Thomas à Becket when he went on his famous embassy to Paris in 1158 caused a scandal because some of his twenty-four magnificent costumes were made of silk. During the early eleventh century several fine new materials appeared, among them velvet, so called from the Latin *villosa*, whence the French *velours*, and a rich stuff made in the Cyclades known as *cyclas,* first used in England for the wide-sleeved vestments worn by the officiating clergy and by the king himself at his coronation. Henry III's coronation robes were described as 'cyclades worked with gold over vestments of silk'.

The French market developed in a totally different manner from the English; it aimed at a luxury trade based on a great deal of expert handwork which was very profitable, since it had as its chief customer an ostentatious court where magnificent clothing was not only desirable but essential, and it exported luxury goods to all the European countries which had no such skilled workers or masters of design.

It was when the French began to travel beyond the Alps that they discovered in Italy a hitherto undreamt-of world of luxury, the magnificence of whose textiles is superbly illustrated in many of Pisanello's drawings of courtiers and court ladies. The French court had been amazed at the splendour of Marie de Medici's trousseaux and that of her attendants when in 1600 she came to marry Henri IV, particularly at the splendid cut-velvet and silk brocades from Genoa. The great statesman Colbert induced Louis XIV to give royal patronage to the silk industry, brought foreign workmen to teach their skills to the weavers at Lyons and on the king's orders they began to make rich silk and gold brocades.

England had no Colbert to encourage a luxury textile industry, nor any court to compare in splendour with that of Versailles; indeed England in the seventeenth century had seen Cromwell's party in power and the Puritan influence cannot be overlooked in the history of English fashion. The English kings (with the exception of Charles II) did not keep a retinue of expensive mistresses who all followed, and sometimes led, the fashion.

After Elizabeth I there were few extravagantly dressed queens of England. Anne of Denmark made over many of Elizabeth's dresses when she became James I's queen, and Henrietta Maria, whose magnificent trousseau was pillaged by her French staff when Charles I insisted that they should return to France, replaced it with far simpler gowns which showed her individual taste. She preferred plain satins to heavy brocades, but also loved fine muslins and laces and kept an army of clear-starchers and laundresses busy maintaining them in perfect order.

Similarly England had no parvenue princesses like those of the Napoleonic era in France to launch new fashions, no Empress Eugénie to spend vast sums of money and most of her time on ordering and displaying her toilettes, no emperors to dictate textile policies, no government to state that it would be to the country's advantage to send fashion abroad because it was a way to rule over others, and no politicians who believed that not only commercial but educational values followed in the footsteps of fashion.

Clothes in the eighteenth century were a passport to society, the wealthy public being admitted to Queen Anne's functions in Kensington Palace provided they were in full dress. In Vienna Joseph II likewise welcomed to his official receptions all citizens suitably attired, for he wished to encourage the new factories and the people to buy new clothes, so their attendance at the public masquerade balls (*Redouten*) was based not on their social status but on their attire.

In France at this time Marie-Antoinette was committing some of the greatest sartorial follies yet seen. Once when her brother Joseph remarked that the magnificent material of her dress must have been very costly, the Queen replied that it had supported several families, and that if she dressed in simple clothes two hundred commercial houses would close. However, when simple muslins took her fancy she did not consider the repercussion on the trade and at the time of her pregnancy began to prefer simpler stuffs, fine batistes and percales. These were not considered sufficiently important to be noted in the lists of her wardrobe, which consisted each year of twelve toilettes for formal occasions, an equal number of less formal

dresses called *de fantaisie* and yet another dozen rich toilettes
which she wore for gaming or supper in the little apartments.

Napoleon continued Colbert's policy of protecting and
developing the French luxury fabric industry and insisted on
Lyons producing rich brocades, heavy velvets and embroidered
silks. So anxious was he that orders should flow into the
textile mills that he liked the women at his court to wear new
dresses all the time and once rebuked the Duchesse d'Abrantès
for appearing in the same dress twice. She was scornful of the
taste of this new plutocracy and complained that dresses were
in Turkish, Greek, Roman or medieval styles – everything
except in good French taste. Napoleon had sent some cashmere
shawls from the orient to Josephine, who at first thought them
hideous and allowed her couturier Leroy to cut up a
magnificent example and make it into a cloak, which infuriated
the Emperor. Soon, however, these shawls became the rage.
Josephine relented and was painted by Prud'hon with a scarlet
one drawn over her knees. Gérard painted Madame Récamier
in a somewhat similar pose and Antoine-Jean Gros Madame
Lucien Bonaparte with a shawl thrown over her shoulders.

The Emperor was determined to include such a sought-after
commodity among home-produced goods and despatched a
librarian from the Bibliothèque Nationale who could speak
oriental languages to central Asia to buy some of the goats
whose pelt was used in the fabulous shawls, and though many
of the 250 animals he acquired died in transport, breeding was
ensured, and 'cashmere' shawls were produced in France far
more cheaply than they could be imported, though the Lyons
shawls were never as good as those of India. Napoleon had all
his own waistcoats and breeches woven from white French
'cashmere' cloth, which he changed every morning, and after
these garments had been washed three or four times threw
them away. Extravagance – or subsidy for home industry, as
one pleases to look at it.

Copies of the cashmere shawls bearing the familiar 'pine
motif' crossed the Channel and were made in Norwich and
Edinburgh until a Scottish manufacturer named Paterson
discovered that highly skilled weaving labour was relatively
cheap in Paisley, and commissioned a number of shawls to be

made there. The workmànship was so good that, through efficient organization, Paisley became the centre of the shawl industry in Britain and eventually gave its name to these copies of an Indian fashion which remained in vogue as long as the crinoline until, with the change to bustles in the 1870s, Paisley shawls vanished from the fashion scene.

Josephine's couturier Leroy was careful to show his patriotism and belief in Napoleon's plans for home industry by ordering lavishly silks from Lyons and woollens from the manufacturers in the north who were trying to produce quality goods previously obtained from England, for now the situation was reversed and it was English techniques which were in advance of Continental ones.

Napoleon therefore decided to recall a weaver called Ternaux, who had fled to England at the time of the Terror. He brought back with him many engineering secrets of spinning and weaving and was eventually created a Baron de l'Empire.

When Charles Worth became the Empress Eugénie's couturier he, like Leroy before him, found himself in a position in which he could dictate to the Lyons mills and decide which materials and colours he wanted. Lyons was then going through a period of depression, for their hand-looms were threatened by the new steam-driven power of English and German manufacture, and Napoleon III, like Napoleon I, insisted that foreign goods should be excluded and home products encouraged. Eugénie, who preferred gowns of tulle and lace, was obliged to appear in magnificent confections of rich Lyons silks and brocades which she called her *robes politiques,* but the ladies of her court followed suit, and so did the rich bourgeoisie, with the result that in the decade of 1860–70 – the years of the crinoline's largest circumference – the number of Lyons silk-looms doubled.

In the meantime science was edging its way into the clothing industry and in 1823 a chemist in Glasgow learned how to cover fabric with a substance which made it waterproof. The garments which have been associated with the name of Charles Macintosh for over a century have their origin in 1495, when some of Columbus's men in Haiti noticed the natives throwing some lumps of a dark-coloured stuff which bounced

up from the ground. This must have been rubber, but little
was done to utilize its peculiar properties until Macintosh
learnt how to cover fabric with it and so make a waterproof
garment. Unfortunately, although it was efficient, it was
also odorous, but in time an improvement was made to
the original formula and 'macintoshes' were marketed with
the mystic letters FFO (Free from Odour) sewn into them.
The only commercial source of this rubber was the South
American continent, and the invention of the pneumatic
tyre and of the internal combustion engine sparked off
there one of the greatest booms in history. A strange city,
Manaus, grew up in the Amazon jungle complete with a huge
opera house, and this luxurious capital flourished until seeds
of the rubber tree were taken via Kew Gardens to Malaya,
where the great rubber fortunes of the early twentieth century
were made. Now the rubberized garment has given way to yet
another scientific invention and coats of plastic vinyl in
brilliant colours or with a moroccan finish are made by
Manleberg, the firm which first made use of Charles
Macintosh's pioneer process.

The influence of art on fashion has always been potent
though usually unacknowledged, and there are remarkably few
textile designers known by name before Poiret, whose highly
individual taste had an immense influence both before and
immediately after the First World War.

During the 1920s one of the most successful links between the
painter and the couturier was Sonia Delaunay, the Russian wife
of the artist Robert, who in 1927 gave an exciting lecture on
the 'Influence of Painting on the Art of Costume' at the
Sorbonne. Two years previously she had opened a small
shop and her designs, all made in materials of her creation,
caused a sensation at the 1925 exhibition of 'Art et Decoration'.
She began selling in quantity to America, but the collapse of
the New York stock market in 1929 ruined her, along with
many other outstanding figures in the fashion world, but did
not prevent her from continuing to work. Now in her eighties,
Sonia Delaunay is recognized as one of the key people of that
period.

Today the international fabric market encircles the globe, and

there is hardly a country, except Russia, which does not
produce its own specialities. The Irish story began in 1950
when some locally made clothes were shown in Dublin to the
visiting Philadelphia Fashion Group of America, whose
members were so struck by their originality that they asked the
designer, then an unknown young girl, to bring her collection
to Philadelphia. Sybil Connolly's success was instantaneous and
store buyers ordered in such quantities that the Dublin
premises had to be entirely reorganized. So had the supply of
native materials, especially the Irish bawneen, a natural white
woollen material previously considered suitable only for tough
country wear. Sybil Connolly persuaded the weavers to supply
this in wider widths and in finer textures and used it for simple
but sophisticated dresses, thus launching the fashion for white.
Ireland now has a thriving export fabric trade and its own shop
in Regent Street, London. The Israeli market is the newest
development and already it produces good woollens, jerseys and
cottons but has not yet attained a personal signature. Scotland
of course continues to be known for (comparatively)
inexpensive woollens, tartans and cashmeres. Switzerland
specializes in the novelty cottons and organdies for which the
house of Fischenbacker is particularly known and which created
the fabulous muslins which were the highlight of the Ungaro
collections in 1967-8. But Switzerland also produces
exquisitely fine silks and Abrahams materials from Zürich can
be found in every Parisian collection of note.

Pure silk staged a come-back from an unexpected source
when after the last war an American soldier who had fought in
the Far East decided to settle in Bangkok. In a few years the
name of Joe Thompson was known in every fashion centre in
the world: he organized the existing haphazard Thai silk
industry into a big business operation which sold to most
important stores and silk dress manufacturers in Europe and
America. He saw that the bolts of material were of the right
width and length required by the trade, that deliveries were
made on time, watched what colours were in fashion, and
styled the stripes and patterns with which some of this
exquisite material was enriched. His house in Bangkok, whose
wide verandahs overlooked a river on the other side of which

were his own weaving-sheds, became a tourist attraction open
to the public, who could see a splendid example of local
architecture filled with treasures, bronzes, stone heads and
carvings, brass hands and bowls. One day he went out for a
stroll and never returned. No trace of his body has ever been
found and his death remains an unsolved mystery.

Although France is still the main source of supply of high-
fashion fabrics it is also the centre of the great textile empire of
Monsieur Boussac who, like Colbert before him, wished to see
France the hub of the textile industries of the world, but
realized that after the war French industry was diminished by
years of German occupation, and that all the inexpensive
cottons which his immense factories could make could
not in the long run be successful unless the world once
again considered France a country of taste and high-fashion.
The result was the foundation of the house of Dior, backed by
the limitless resources of the Tissus Boussac, and the
re-emergence of France as the leader of fashion.

6 The fashion creators

The most important customers of these international fabric manufacturers are the Parisian couturiers, who set the trend for a world-wide trade and whose choice has an immense influence on the type of material which becomes fashionable.

The demise of the Parisian *haute couture* market has been predicted ever since the collapse of the American stock exchange in the autumn of 1929 when the massive bi-annual injection of American dollars ceased. Not only were there thousands of people in the United States penniless but also thousands in Europe without markets for their skills. In Paris alone 10,000 workers became unemployed in firms connected with fashion and at the same time the tourist trade diminished until by 1934 the number of Americans visiting France had fallen by a quarter.

The Second World War was considered to be the death-blow of *haute couture* and few people in 1945, either in Europe or America, thought Paris could ever recapture its position of world authority on fashion. The glittering world of the 1920s, when France's position in the fashion world seemed unassailable, appeared to have vanished for ever: in 1929 fashion was second in importance in France's exports; ten years later it had fallen to twenty-seventh.

During the war the Americans had announced that they could do without French models, and after four years of good business without recourse to Paris the American designers believed they had found their own style. This proved not to be the case and in due course the buyers, together with their 'commissionaires', who had greatly suffered from the loss of their most important clients, came back to Paris but followed a very different procedure. Instead of buying a number of fully finished models from the collections they bought *toiles*, i.e. patterns in holland of the model which give away the secret of the cut, and were accompanied by references for the fabric and all trimmings. The various firms then made up the models in their own workrooms, though sometimes several firms clubbed together and, if they bought the made-up model, organized a coast-to-coast promotion, which meant that an important store in each of the main cities, New York, Chicago, Los Angeles or San Francisco, would share a model which the couturier in question agreed should not be sold to any other firm in the same city. Buyers still bought a certain number of complete models but their purchases in 1962, though far from negligible, could not compare with the pre-war spending when in 1925 American orders alone accounted for no less than £17 million pounds.

The post-war women no longer had the time to spend searching and being fitted for the most elegant clothes, nor were there the same number of elegant soirées and resorts where they could be displayed; also the post-war *nouveaux riches* were terrified of being classed as such, England had always been a small customer for luxury goods, and the rest of Europe was in chaos. Nevertheless Paris revived and though it now has many rivals remains the largest fashion mart of the world.

The creation of the *haute couture* is often attributed to Charles Worth, but though he developed the immense possibilities of an expanding market, the trade of selling models to foreign countries, carrying with them a demand for French fabrics, had been in existence for centuries. Worth was a good business man as well as a brilliant designer and took every advantage of the rapidly developing international trade of the late nineteenth century, but behind him lay a long history of business acumen and a carefully nurtured craft tradition. French fashions had been exported for hundreds of years before Worth's day: as long ago as the fourteenth century it was the practice to

send dolls dressed in the latest fashion from Paris to the courts
of Europe to acquaint them with the newest mode and create
a demand for French fabrics. When the seven-year-old Isabella
of France came to England to become the second wife of
Richard II she was sent some fashionably dressed dolls from
France, some large enough for her to make use of the clothes,
others smaller for her to play with, but dressed in a manner
which showed how her own clothes should be constructed.

In 1497 when a life-sized doll was ordered by Queen Anne
of Brittany as a gift for Queen Isabella of Castille it was at
first considered inelegant by the fashion judges and had to be
re-dressed before it was despatched. Isabella d'Este Gonzaga,
Marchioness of Mantua, one of the most cultured women of her
time, had sent to her wooden dolls dressed in the latest fashion
from France, and when Marie de Medici was about to marry
Henry IV of France he sent several model dolls to her to show
how the ladies of the court she was soon to lead were dressed.

Later in the seventeenth century the dolls, usually half-size,
were exposed at the Hôtel de Rambouillet before replicas were
despatched to the various courts of Europe and the *précieuses* of
the time, among them Mademoiselle de Scudéry, were called
upon to advise on their dressing.

In the eighteenth century it became popular to send abroad
a pair of dolls, one dressed *en grande toilette* and the other *en
déshabille,* called Grande Pandore and Petite Pandore, and these
fashion dolls, or pandoras, became a recognized method of
distributing French fashions throughout Europe. So
important were they considered that even when countries were
at war the fashion dolls were given safe-conducts, and in 1704
the abbé Provost commented on an act of gallantry 'which is
worthy of being noted in the chronicles of history: for the
benefit of the ladies, the ministers of both courts granted a
special pass to the mannequin'. That pass was always respected,
and during the time of the greatest enmity on both sides the
mannequin was the one object which remained unmolested.
The free pass for the *Grande Poupée* ceased at the end of the
First Empire, for by that time the fashion-plate had arrived to
take its place.

All Europe looked to the pandoras to tell them what was the

latest mode and these ambassadors of fashion not only carried
the French style all over Europe but acted as a show window
for the textile trade and the hundred and one falbalas for which
France was famous. They also advertised the art of coiffure;
Madame de Sévigné, in the seventeenth century, had had one
made specially for her daughter, who lived in the country, to
show her how to dress her hair, and in 1763 Paris had an
exhibition of some thirty dolls which showed the latest
hairdressing styles. Marie-Antoinette ordered fashion dolls
from Rose Bertin when she wanted to acquaint her mother and
sisters in Vienna of the latest Paris fashions, and Rose Bertin's
dolls were so famous that during the Terror, when she escaped
to London, she continued to send them to the various courts of
Europe.

Rose Bertin was born Marie-Jean Bertin at Abbeville in
northern France of poor but respectable parents, her father a
postman, her mother a nurse. She had little education but must
have been good with her needle, for when she was sixteen and
came to Paris to try her fortune she was fortunate enough to get
employment at the 'Trait Galant', a *maison de modes* kept by
Mademoiselle Pagelle. Almost immediately fate took a hand:
she was sent with the *corbeille* for two important young ladies
to the house of their formidable relative the old Princesse de
Conti, and in a dark room she mistook the Princess for her
waiting-woman, talked to her familiarly and showed her the
dresses. The old Princess took a fancy to the young girl and
when one of the richest heiresses of France was about to
marry the Duc de Chartres she arranged that the entire
trousseau should be made at the 'Trait Galant'. The young
duchess became Rose's most important customer and eventually
made it possible for her to set up her own establishment in the
Rue St-Honoré, which she called 'Au Grand Mogul' after the
fashion for all things Turkish. The Duchesse de Chartres
introduced her widowed sister-in-law, the pretty Princesse de
Lamballe, to her modiste and between them they managed to
present her to the Dauphine, Marie-Antoinette. This was done
not without difficulty, because royalty did not meet commoners
of Rose's class. It was a propitious moment, for at about this
time the Austrian Ambassador at Versailles had written to the

Empress Maria Theresa that her daughter was not paying
sufficient attention to her appearance, but with the advent of
Rose, young, enthusiastic and ambitious, the picture changed and
soon the Austrian princess became imbued with the desire to
dazzle the world with her toilettes. In this Marie-Antoinette
succeeded brilliantly, and two years later when she sent her
mother a portrait of herself the Empress sarcastically remarked
that it was the picture of an actress, not of the future Queen of
France. In 1774 Louis XV died and Marie-Antoinette, now
Queen, bored by the strict etiquette of the French court,
neglected by her husband, and with no prospect of producing the
longed-for heir, turned more and more to the distractions of
chiffons. Her twice-weekly sessions with Rose always brought
something new and amusing and between them they encouraged
the deplorable fashion of the high and intricate head-dresses.
The Austrian Empress again wrote anxiously to her daughter,
saying that she had heard her head-gear rose some 36 inches
from the roots of the hair and was built up into a tower
with countless feathers and ribbons. These extraordinary
head-dresses soon became the subject for the satirists of
the day and were scarcely less ridiculous than those of Mary
Darly's caricatures. Madame de Campan, the Queen's devoted
lady-in-waiting, considered Rose Bertin as the prime influence
in making Marie-Antoinette so spendthrift and frivolous
and there is little doubt that this was so but, during the few
years when these ridiculous head-dresses were fashionable,
Marie-Antoinette was in her early twenties and Rose not yet
thirty. It is not surprising that Mademoiselle Bertin should
have become puffed up with conceit, for in ten years she, a
provincial nobody, had won a unique position in the world:
she was elected one of the two syndics of the new corporation
of the Marchands de Modes formed in 1776, she featured as an
allegorical figure in a contemporary play and was honoured by
a poet of the period, Jacques Delille, who praises Fashion
because it embellishes nature.

He says:
  Quand Bertin fait briller son goût industrieux
  L'Etoffe obéissante en cent formes se joue,

Se développe en châle, en ceinture se noue ;
Du pinceau son aiguille emprunte des couleurs,
Brille de diamants, se nuance de fleurs,
En longs replis flottants fait ondoyer sa moire,
Donne un voile à l'Amour, une écharpe à la gloire . . .

The modiste was given the entrée into the royal antechamber
without demanding permission from anyone, she was paid
more than a secretary of state and her clients included not only
the cream of French aristocracy but also the Queens of Spain
and Sweden, the Duchess of Devonshire and the Duchess of
Württemberg, later Czarina of Russia.

The political climate in France was changing at this time, the
country was on the verge of bankruptcy, but the cynicism of
the court and its hangers-on was such that when a bad harvest
brought about a shortage of bread and the bakers' shops were
stormed a *bonnet à la révolte* came out the same day; when the
scandal of the Queen's necklace was at its height, a hat adorned
with strings of pearls appeared dubbed *au collier de la reine* and
another, a straw hat with purple ribbons, was called *cardinal
sur la paille* in memory of the Cardinal de Rohan who, because
of the part he had played in that tangled story, now lay on
straw in the Bastille.

Even the change to a simpler fashion did not diminish Rose's
bills, and during the nineteen months immediately before the royal
couple's attempted escape the Queen ordered from Mademoiselle
Bertin no fewer than forty poufs and fifty bonnets.

There were rumours of Rose's bankruptcy, possibly put out
by her increasing number of enemies, but no proof has ever
been found of this. In July 1792 she left Paris with four
employees and fifteen cases filled with models and materials
and was reported to have sold 'spangled fripperies' at a
high price in Frankfurt. Later in the year she moved to
London, where many of her old clients were already installed,
but they were penniless émigrés and it was with the wealthy
English that she did successful business. She also corresponded
with clients in foreign countries and endeavoured to have
the money from outstanding accounts sent to England.
Her name appeared on a list of proscribed émigrés and

her business in Paris and her house at Epernay were
sequestered, but she managed to extricate herself from this
dilemma by stating, not without reason, that she, an honest
hard-working woman, had not been paid by many of her
aristocratic clients, and was obliged to go abroad to sell her
wares and talent.

She visited Germany and Russia in 1797 where the Czarina,
who had been a good customer in Paris, patronized her and
where she had many other clients from the past. At home her
nephew continued to run the business, and as late as 1808
Rose supplied the Queen of Spain with six magnificent fans
and a silver tissue gown, but in 1812 she sold the shop and
retired to her beloved Epernay, where she died peacefully,
having lived to see Napoleon begin his march to destruction
in Russia.

Rose's successor as principal French modiste had already
been noted and complimented by her one evening at the Opéra
when she commented on the coiffure of one of the actresses and
asked the name of its creator. This turned out to be Louis
Hippolyte Leroy, whose father was a stage hand at the Opéra
but who had high ambitions. Born in 1763, he had grown to
manhood when Louis XVI and Marie-Antoinette were still on
the throne and insisted on wearing the aristocratic costume of
silk coat, velvet collar, embroidered satin waistcoat, pointed
shoes and powdered wig even during the Revolution, when he
openly deplored the lack of chic and drab dress of those
terrible years. Possibly this may have given rise to the rumour
that he was a Royalist and, understandably, he was appalled
when a summons came for him to appear before the Convention.
To his immense relief he found this august committee wanted
his help in designing a suitable costume for the glorious
Republicans. Leroy's allegiance to the Royalist cause and
costume changed overnight as he realized the possibilities
offered him by this parvenu class who, immensely rich from
army contracts or deals in the proscribed estates of the émigrés
but unsure of their own taste, would willingly follow his
suggestions and pay him generously, and soon he was in his
element.

Leroy's shrewdness made him realize that Josephine was – or

might become – an important client and he wooed her servants with small gifts until she finally received him. In turn she introduced him to the *Merveilleuses* and it was through their favour that he became the dictator of fashion. This was a very different proposition from the heyday of Mademoiselle Bertin, when for nearly two decades the style of the dress changed hardly at all and it was the fichus, ribbons, flowers, paniers, draperies, poufs and head-dresses which gave the toilette variety and personal distinction. Previously, though the Lyons mills had provided most of the silk, other materials were imported from every country; now, owing to Napoleon's chauvinistic policy, every yard of fabric and every accessory had to be made in France. After the disappearance of the hoop skirts and the paniers the styles changed rapidly and the would-be classical gown of the Directoire and the Empire demanded a totally different cut and type of material.

Leroy saw himself as the sole creator of French fashion and was greatly disappointed when Napoleon commissioned Isabey, a pupil of Louis David's, to design the coronation robes. It required all Josephine's entreaties to make him carry out someone else's designs but he proved a brilliant collaborator. Isabey's stiff drawings showed no comprehension of the materials required but Leroy's knowledge and taste transformed these dull sketches into sumptuous garments of smooth satins and velvets, soft, novel and magnificently embroidered. The *metteur en scène* for the whole coronation was David himself, whose immense canvas of the ceremony, now in the Louvre, shows clearly the lovely costumes all designed by Isabey but carried out by Leroy.

After this success there was no doubt that Leroy was the leading dress-designer. He managed to give variety and individuality to the slight Empire dresses composed of thin materials and his choice of colours and embroideries was outstanding. A fashion article describes with delight 'white muslin dresses worn over blue, yellow or pale pink taffeta, embroidered white upon white, worn with shawls of genuine or imitation cashmere'.

Like Rose Bertin, he was known throughout Europe and sent his representatives, then known as *factrices*, to the courts of Spain, Bavaria, Sweden and Naples as well as to the lovely Princess Borghese, Napoleon's sister Pauline, in Rome. In a picture at Versailles she is seen wearing one of his dresses consisting of a blue wrap over white satin, the dress embroidered with gold flowers and edged with gold fringes, a cameo of Napoleon on the diamond-studded belt.

Leroy continued faithful to Josephine after her banishment to Malmaison but he also worked for Marie-Louise. Like her Austrian predecessor, Marie-Antoinette, Marie-Louise arrived in Paris quite indifferent to clothes but later, when she fell in love with Monsieur de Neipberg (whom she married after Napoleon's death), she became clothes-mad and wrote to Leroy ordering dozens of dresses, hats and *déshabillés* to be sent to her in Vienna.

After the fall of Napoleon and the return of the Bourbons Leroy found himself working once again with members of the old aristocracy who had formed his taste, and Marie-Antoinette's daughter re-entered Paris wearing one of Leroy's dresses.

Leroy outlived Napoleon as Bertin had outlived Marie-Antoinette: he also outlived the style of which he had been the master. Although he was commissioned to design the robes for the coronation of Charles X, his day was over and he produced nothing but a banal echo of the past. He made his business over to his niece and died in 1829, a forgotten man.

Either because there were so many social or political upheavals, or because no one of sufficient talent emerged, there were few top fashion figures between the 1820s when Leroy retired and the rise of Worth in the 1860s, though three women made names for themselves: Palmyre and Vignon, who were responsible for the Empress Eugénie's wardrobe before the advent of Worth, and Victorine, whose creations are mentioned by Balzac and praised by Stendhal.

Charles Frederick Worth came of an obscure family in Lincolnshire. His father gambled away the little his profession of a lawyer brought in and the son's schooldays were interrupted by the necessity of earning something to help support the family. At 11 Charles Frederick was working in a printing works, at 13 he had become a cashier in the London firm of Lewis & Allenby which sold materials and coats and where he

learned the discipline necessary for any solid achievement in
the world of commerce. He was also within easy walking
distance of the National Gallery where, looking at the portraits,
he was astounded by the magnificence of the clothes created in
periods when the many new methods of the nineteenth century
which made splendour a comparatively easy achievement were
unknown.

Worth decided to seek work in Paris, where he arrived as a
complete stranger, speaking no French, and with only a few
shillings in his pocket. He soon obtained work at the Maison
Gagelin, which was obviously a house of high repute for its
name appears frequently in *La Sylphide*, a paper recently
founded by Emile de Girardin to which such eminent writers
as Dumas, Théophile Gautier and Balzac contributed. During
the twelve years Charles Worth worked for this firm his
technical capabilities and taste were developed by the beauty
and variety which Paris fashion offered. There was one thing
only he could give Paris in return, and that was his English
knowledge of cut. In this sphere he effected great reforms,
training his underlings in the technique of the run of the
cloth, an expertise which has paid dividends in every period
ever since the days of the Plantagenets.

An important event in Worth's life was the Great Exhibition
of 1851 in the Crystal Palace which Paxton had constructed
in Hyde Park, and where exhibits from the Maison Gagelin sold
more than 350,000 francs' worth to leading houses abroad and
won the only gold medal awarded to France. The next
important exhibition, the 1855 World Fair in Paris, brought
Charles Worth his first personal triumph when his design for a
court train won first prize.

At this time Worth arranged to sell some of the models he
had designed for the Maison Gagelin to foreign buyers with
the permission to copy them, together with details of where
the necessary materials could be obtained. This business
arrangement, so obviously beneficial to French trade, is usually
referred to as the beginning of the international fashion
market though, as we have seen, a similar practice had been
followed for some hundreds of years.

Following this success Worth persuaded his firm to set up a

department of ready-made clothes, and he also persuaded a pretty young girl who was employed as a saleswoman to marry him. The young *ménage* was happy and successful, and so was the business, but the older partners had become hidebound in their own period and were incapable of developing in the manner suggested by Worth, who now left Gagelin and, together with a Swede named Otto Bobergh, formed a new company.

The Swede soon disappeared from history, but Charles Worth's flair for success led him to take premises at 7 Rue de la Paix, above which lived his family, at a time when that street was in a quiet residential quarter, but soon afterwards a great square nearby was cleared and an Opera House built there, thus making a new and exciting centre for Parisian society. The fashion houses in the Rue Richelieu saw with dismay that the smart world was driving westwards and abandoning the old centre of the mode.

The story of Worth's introduction to the court of the Empress Eugénie is well known. The wife of the Austrian Ambassador was Princess Pauline Metternich, whose dark colouring and thin figure would be admired today but who, although described by the Princess Mathilde, the Emperor's cousin, as 'a little histrionic monkey with her thirty-six flounces and her forty trunks', was always outstandingly well dressed. Worth had already insinuated himself into the Princess's *entourage* by sending his wife with a sheaf of sketches which she managed to show to the Princess, saying that she could name her price for whichever of the designs pleased her. Pauline's first dress from Worth was of silver-threaded white tulle with bunches of pink cowslips half hidden in tufts of grass, and a broad white satin sash to emphasize her tiny waist. To this the Princess added a wealth of diamonds sparkling like dew among the spring flowers so that the lovely creation naturally caught the Empress's eye. She asked the name of the Princess Metternich's dressmaker and from that moment Worth was made – and Pauline had to pay higher prices in future for her own toilettes.

Worth's invitation to the Tuileries was the fulfilment of his desires, now he had as a client one of the most beautiful women of her day, an empress with unlimited money to spend who was a world-wide advertisement of his work. His flair for providing the right frame for any individual woman became legendary. When Madame Octave Feuillet, wife of the novelist and playwright, came to Paris to be presented at court she realized the day before the ceremony that her dress was a disaster, so she rose early next morning, went to Worth's house and insisted on the master being awakened. She explained to the dressing-gowned couturier her dilemma, he ushered her into his wife's bedroom, where poor Marie was not yet dressed, and, looking at the shrinking form of the wretched client, appeared to dream a dream. Then he sent for materials and his première and set to work. By the evening the dress was ready, a dream such as the creator had imagined and the client hoped for – and Madame Feuillet had the happiness of having her toilette remarked on by the Empress.

The extravagance of Eugénie's court rivalled that of Josephine's or Marie-Antoinette's and the director of the Louvre wryly remarked that his annual grant for purchases was 7,000 francs whereas the Empress received 100,000 francs a month for her clothes.

Everybody who was anybody wanted to be dressed by Worth not only for contemporary clothes but also for the many fancy-dress balls which were part of the social round and cost the court immense sums of money. He composed a silver lamé dress for the Duchesse de Morny as the Morning Star, a feathered dress which turned the Baronne de Rothschild into a Bird of Paradise, and for 'la Castiglione' he designed a superb Queen of the Night costume in black velvet with long panels strewn with silver stars edged with silver fringe and a coronet of stars on a black ground which encircled her head. But most famous of all Worth's fancy dresses was the peacock gown he contrived for the Princesse de Sagan which had a long green velvet train edged with the eyes of peacock's feathers and a tulle skirt draped over a sky blue satin crinoline dotted with stars, and on her head a peacock's head with a long veil behind.

Worth also designed for the theatre and during the Paris Exhibition of 1867 he dressed the ravishing Hortense Schneider, star of Offenbach's new operetta *La Grande Duchesse de*

Gerolstein, and made for her a dashing outfit which had a hussar's braided jacket slung across her shoulders and an osprey in her matching braid-embroidered velvet cap.

When the war of 1870 broke out Worth's firm closed and his house was used as a hospital but after the armistice he returned and revived new fashions, but although there were once more official *fêtes* and receptions, a beautiful empress no longer presided over them. Worth now developed the slender polonaise with a draped overskirt or tunic and though he was relieved the crinoline was at last extinct, for he had become heartily tired of it, these complicated arrangements of two or three different materials looped, pleated, frilled and gathered into monstrous steatopygous figures could not be considered a happy replacement. He made one more contribution to fashion when he launched the small 'crinolette' of steel which held out the skirts at the back but was flat in front. It was greeted by the jingle:

> 'Who's responsible, I ask you,
> For this strange portentous birth
> Of an ancient Hideous fashion?
> And an echo answers: Worth. . . .'

Worth was always superstitious; he particularly feared 10th March and it was on that day in 1895 that he died, leaving his two sons, Jean-Philippe and Gaston, to carry on the business. They made all Eleanora Duse's clothes both on and off the stage for thirty years and Jean-Philippe had a close and tender concern for this beautiful and talented woman who once wrote: 'If you do not help me, the magic leaves my roles'. The house of Worth continued into the third generation under the founder's grandson Jacques, who was awarded the Légion d'Honneur, and did not close its doors until 1956, just a hundred years after its founder's first great success.

Two other Englishmen played a considerable role in Paris fashion: Charles Creed and Redfern. The latter's real name was Charles Poynter but he came to Paris as a representative of the London House of Redfern, founded in 1842, which numbered Queen Victoria among its clients, and opened a branch of the English firm in the Rue de Rivoli. Redfern's great innovation was the tailor-made, so often attributed to Paul Poiret, which he introduced to Parisians, and this essentially English garment still remains part of many women's wardrobe. The classical distinction and severe cut of Redfern's day-clothes were complemented by his imaginative stage costumes and when he dressed Mary Garden in the musical drama *Aphrodite* (adapted from Pierre Louys's novel) he transformed the young American into a beautiful Tanagra figure.

The other Englishman who made an impact on the Parisian scene was the tailor Creed, who was recommended to the Empress Eugénie by Queen Victoria as a maker of riding habits. Eugénie de Montijo was a magnificent horsewoman and it was on horse-back that the Emperor first saw and fell in love with her, so she attached the greatest importance to the perfect fit of her habits. Her choice of Creed as her tailor made his fortune and was responsible for founding the house in the Rue de la Paix which continued under his sons and grandsons until the last war, when Charles Creed, Parisian-born and trained, founded a couture house in London which he directed until his death in 1966, and a wholesale firm bearing his name still exists.

One of the most famous of the early French couture houses was that of Jacques Doucet, the son of Edouard Doucet who opened a shop in the Rue de la Paix in 1824 which then dealt solely in ladies' laces and ribbons and gentlemen's shirts and cravats. Edouard Doucet soon found this latter department grew in importance as men's dress became more stereotyped and therefore such details as ruffles and frills, relics of the defunct *jabot*, required especial attention. In those days the *beaux* considered that only in England could their cravats be properly bleached and starched and sent them across the Channel to be laundered, until Doucet had the idea of installing on his premises a laundry for fine linen run on British lines.

At an early age Doucet's only son Jacques evinced a great interest in fashion and not long after the Franco-Prussian War he opened a new department in his father's house for ladies' dresses which was an immediate success. Jacques Doucet's love and knowledge of French eighteenth-century art was translated in his professional life into delicate toilettes of real beauty, and in his private life into a house exquisitely furnished with pieces by Reisener, Leleu and other masters of the *grand siècle*. He formed an art and archeological library which is now one of the treasures of Paris and built up a magnificent collection of eighteenth-century paintings; nevertheless he was so much in tune with all that was happening in the world of art that when the new century produced such men as Cézanne, Picasso, Matisse and Braque he bought their canvases when they were still unknown. Picasso's famous *Demoiselles d'Avignon*, now in the Metropolitan Museum of Art in New York, once hung in his hall, and Douanier Rousseau's *Joueuse de Flûte*, which he left to the Louvre, was in his study. He sold all his Bouchers, Fragonards, Chardins and Guardis and made a new setting in the contemporary style, every bit as elegant as his previous eighteenth-century *décor*.

At the Great Exhibition of 1900 in Paris Doucet, Paquin, Callot Soeurs, the Worth brothers and Redfern were all asked to exhibit. Jean-Philippe and Gaston Worth wished to show their models on life-like wax figures set in scenes suited to their costumes, such as Longchamps race-course or an evening at the Opéra, but their colleagues found this new idea too bizarre and not in keeping with the rest of the exhibits so the brothers leased a corner of a separate pavilion where they displayed scenes of everyday life, from a lady's maid to a fashionable lady dressed in expensive court finery, which caused so much interest by its novelty that the police had to be called in to protect the precious exhibits.

Madame Paquin, the first woman since Rose Bertin to achieve a top position in Paris fashion, was president of the fashion section of the Exhibition and for her display a beautifully dressed wax figure of herself was shown seated in front of her own toilet-table set with silver. She had opened her dress salon nine years earlier and was her own *mannequin de ville,* appearing at the races, at Trouville Casino and at all important Parisian functions dressed in the height of fashion. She was particularly known for her blue serge costumes, an English vogue which then had the highest *cachet* and which she enlivened with braid and gold buttons, but was equally famous for her luxurious evening gowns shimmering in gold and silver

which the jealous Poiret attributed to her Levantine origin.
Unlike most women and most couturiers, she was a first-class
organizer and (with a banker husband to guide her) founded
the first foreign branches of a Paris house abroad, opening one
in London in 1912, followed by others in Buenos Aires and
Madrid. She sent ten mannequins dressed in the same model to
the races and her fashion shows antedated Courrèges by ending
each collection with a score of girls, all dressed in white, who
performed a kind of ballet.

Four other women at the turn of the century made a mark in
the Paris couture, Madame Cheruit and the three Callot sisters.
This firm shared with Doucet a love of the rococo fashions of
the eighteenth century, the falbalas of ribbons and lace which
went so well with the elaborate fashions of the early twentieth
century, and they persuaded the firm of Coudurier-Fructus to
reproduce magnificent but supple gold lamés specially for their
use. Soon their premises in the Rue Taitbout became too small
for their expanding business and they were the first couturiers
to move to the then far away Avenue Matignon. Madame
Cheruit, originally employed by the fashion house of Raudnitz
(founded in 1873), later installed herself in a lovely old *hôtel* in
the Place Vendôme. Unlike her other rivals, Madame Cheruit, a
striking personality, insisted on simple, austere models and
disliked the elaborate fashions of her day. Poiret gives an
excellent description of her at his first interview when this
supremely elegant woman was wearing a plain dark blue dress
with a very high collar rising up to her ears and edged with a
white ruche into which was set her lovely face.

Also in the Place Vendôme was Doeuillet who had started
his career with Callot Soeurs. He is said to have been the first
to inaugurate the fashion mannequin parade, as opposed to the
usual method of the girls wandering about in the salons, or
dressing up in any particular type of dress which the client
wished to see. In 1928, when the collapse of the American
market was imminent, he joined forces with Doucet, now an
old man, and formed the house of Doeuillet-Doucet.

With the turn of the century a new spirit began to invade
both the arts and the applied art of fashion. During the first
few years Paris acclaimed Isadora Duncan dancing in a brief

peplum and bare feet, the first exhibition (1905) of the painters
nicknamed *les Fauves* because of the wild exuberance of their
colours, the first performance of the Russian ballet presented
by Diaghilev (1909), with settings and costumes by Léon Bakst.
None of these novelties showed any trace of the dainty
sweet-pea colours and fine laces beloved of the generously
formed but sternly corseted Edwardians, none of them accorded
with the 'latest Paris fashions', but they made an indelible
impression on young Paul Poiret to whom Jacques Doucet
had given his first engagement. Paul Poiret had shown his
sketches to Madame Cheruit with no success; now he was
encouraged by the *grand seigneur* of the mode who thought
the young man had taste, but his path was not yet clear, for
the *vendeuses* were firmly opposed to his designs of simple
dresses in straight, almost classic lines which they contended
were not only what their customers were not used to and did
not want, but for which they could not possibly ask the sums
of money usually demanded for the elaborately boned, lined,
petticoated, lace-frilled models typical of the day. For a
short time Poiret had a situation with Worth, then in 1904 with
a tiny capital sum given him by his mother he opened a small
shop in the Rue Auber, near the new Opera House, with only
eight employees. Here everything was totally unlike anything
ever seen elsewhere, and Poiret's window displays, which he
created himself, the first imaginative ones to be seen in Paris,
caused all passers-by to stop and stare.

The vivid colours of *les Fauves* and the *Ballet Russe* appeared
in Poiret's clothes, which were shorn of all superfluities of
trimming. He refused to allow his clients to wear corsets and
advocated straight dresses which fell in graceful folds to the
feet. Two young artists became his friends, Georges Lepape
and Paul Iribe. The latter's book *Les Robes de Paul Poiret
racontées par Paul Iribe* is now a collector's piece but although it
came out in 1908 a large important volume entitled *Les
Créateurs de la Mode*, which appeared two years later, listed
Callot Soeurs, Mesdames Cheruit and Georgette, Béchoff-David,
Doeuillet, Doucet, Martial et Armand and Worth – but did not
mention Poiret.

Copies of Iribe's book were sent by Poiret to the crowned

heads of Europe, all of whom replied courteously except the Queen of England, who requested that in future he would refrain from addressing such matter to her. Poiret was the first person to substitute the living mannequin for the wooden dummy on which hitherto clothes had been made, and spent much time and trouble in grooming and teaching the girls to display with an apparently effortless art his striking models. In 1911 he set out with nine mannequins to tour the capitals of Europe. The nine girls were all dressed in a specially designed uniform of a blue serge coat and skirt with cloaks in reversible plaid, and on their heads wore oilcloth hats with an embroidered 'P'. The entire party travelled in two cars of vast size while the secretary-general travelled ahead by rail with the dresses, and arranged the hotel accommodation which Poiret insisted should all be on the same floor, with himself at one end of the passage and the secretary at the other to discourage the attentions of young men. Nor would he permit the girls to receive any presents; nothing was allowed, neither flowers, bonbons, *billets doux* nor banknotes, for the honour of the house of Poiret was incompatible with such liberties. In each capital the demonstrations, as Poiret called the dress parades, took place before crowned heads and the nobility, and the troupe was besieged by journalists and received massive publicity.

Poiret's influence was not limited to his fashion work but permeated all branches of interior decoration. When he visited the Vienna *Werkstätte* he was impressed by the close contact between the artisan and the artist and on his return to Paris opened a studio for the creation of furniture and other household accessories, naming this department after his elder daughter, Martine. His interiors with their memories of Bakst's brilliant *Ballet Russe* settings are redolent of the world of luxury he loved, and their pinks and purples, tasselled cushions and curved lampshades all recall his period and his astonishing personality. He was the first couturier to market a perfume under his label, called after his second daughter, Rosine, a gimmick which has become a financial safeguard to more than one modern couturier.

L'époque Poiret was indisputably one of the richest periods of original art in both dress and *décor* and Poiret left a far greater

57 Diaphanous muslin dresses became fashionable at the time of the Directory, when Louis-Leopold Boilly painted this charming picture of the wife and daughters of Christophe-Philippe Oberkampf, one of the first French manufacturers to produce imitations of Indian muslins. Collection Montcel.

58 Switzerland is the home of the finest muslin goods and the name of Christian Fischbacher associated with the most original varieties of this material, many of which are featured every season in the Paris collections. In 1968 Ungaro made this pant-suit from a Fischbacher cotton enriched with raised stripes and spots. Photo Kublin.

59 What could be more attractive than white
muslin ruffles edged with black? So thought a
lady of this century's first decade when she
dressed for the races or a garden party in a long
frilled skirt and a large flower-decorated hat.
Picture by Caro Delvaille. Photograph by
Roger-Viollet, Paris.

60 The same motif was exploited in a model by
Yves St-Laurent in 1968, when the sleeves were
suppressed, the shoulders emphasized and the skirt
no longer swept the floor. Reproduced by
permission of Yves St-Laurent.

61 The ultimate in elaboration was reached during the Second Empire when the Belgian artist Alfred Stevens painted 'La Dame en Rose' pensively examining one of her bibelots, dressed in a trailing muslin gown entirely composed of thousands of tiny tucks and narrow lace frills. Archives Photographiques, Paris.

62 A far simpler version of the muslin dress was designed by Bellevile et Cie of London in 1968. There are no frills, the neck is still high and the sleeves long, but the skirt is of medium width and barely reaches the ankles, though it is liberally sprinkled with posies of flowers. Reproduced by courtesy of *Vogue*.

63 In the late eighteenth century the Lyons mills produced materials which rivalled in beauty of weave, colour and design those of the oriental silks which for centuries had been the envy of western weavers. Madame Adelaide was painted by Labille-Guiard wearing a magnificent costume composed of a variety of plain and patterned taffetas enriched by ribbons.

64 The boldly patterned black and white silk of John Cavanagh's silk dress with its severe bloused top and slender skirt dates from 1960. Photograph by Michael Williams.

65 In 1967 the Scotch firm Hogg of
Hawick posed the newly popular model,
Twiggy, in one of their patterned
pullovers whose design clearly derives
from William Morris, as does the silk of
John Cavanagh's dress. Photograph by
John Adrian, reproduced by courtesy of
Hogg of Hawick.

66 In the summer of 1925 a short evening
gown in a bold black and white design
presented a formula which has continued
popular through the subsequent decades.
Equally slender but made in an unpatterned
material was the white satin dress with its
three tiers of fluttering points worn by the
Baroness de Rothschild. Reproduced by
courtesy of *Vogue*.

67 In 1967 Patrick de Barentzen of Rome
designed an afternoon dress in a large
patterned black and white design which
closely resembled the effect achieved in 1925
but gave his model sleeves, a high
décolletage and a wide-brimmed off-face
hat. Photo Gisela, reproduced by courtesy
of the *Sunday Times*.

68 Three years after the Baroness de Rothschild wore her petal-pointed white satin gown Louiseboulanger innovated the short-in-front, low-at-the-back line, and one of her most successful models is shown on the left, its skirt panels cut-on-the-cross, its slender bodice silhouetted against an outsize white ostrich fan. Reproduced by courtesy of *Vogue*.

69 The boldly patterned black and white material first successful in the Twenties was used in 1968 by Yves St-Laurent to create one of the waistless, loose-fitting, long-sleeved dresses typical of his very individual style. Photograph reproduced by courtesy of Tissus Abraham et Cie.

70 Few figures in the fashion world have become as familiar to posterity as Rose Bertin, Marie-Antoinette's modiste. Her portrait, after Trinquesse, was painted when her youthful good looks were already blurred by the heavy chin which often accompanies the high living of success. Reproduced by courtesy of *Apollo* magazine.

CHÉR   PAQUIN

71 After the First World War skirts stopped short several inches above the ankles and both Cheruit (left) and Paquin (right) made simple dinner dresses in fragile materials with moderate *décolletages* and short transparent sleeves trimmed with cascades of lace, a sash or ribbon bows. Buckled shoes were de rigueur and hair was piled high with tiny curls flat on the cheeks. Photographs by Colomb-Gerard, Paris.

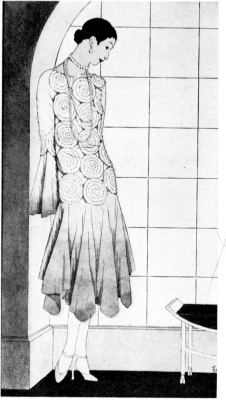

72 In 1926 skirts were uniformly short and often pleated. Chanel, Lelong and Cheruit all played variations on the theme of pleated skirts and hip-length jumpers or jackets, with a strong preference for nautical stripes or geometric designs. Hats were head-hugging cloches and shoes tan-coloured, or tan and white. Reproduced by courtesy of *Vogue*.

73 The name of Vionnet was intimately connected with the bias cut, and the intricacy and perfection of her workmanship conceded to be the finest in Paris. A deceptively simple dinner dress of 1925 has a petal-pointed skirt and a bodice composed of whorls of the same pastel shaded chiffon. Reproduced by courtesy of *Vogue*.

74 Norman Hartnell (above) was the first London couturier since Reville to make a name for himself, and by the early Thirties, when this photograph was taken, was dressing most of the young beauties of the day. His slender, draped dresses were shown to advantage by lovely Margaret Vyner, later wife of the dramatist Hugh Williams who died so tragically in 1970, seen here in a clinging draped gown of soft crêpe, with many jewelled bracelets worn over the long, tight sleeves. Photographs by Fayer, reproduced by courtesy of Norman Hartnell.

75 Edward Molyneux (above) was already installed and successful in Paris in the mid Twenties and a decade later opened a London branch in Grosvenor Street. In 1934 he made the trousseau for Princess Marina when she married the Duke of Kent, among which was this elegant evening dress and wrap made of satin trimmed with ostrich feathers sent to her as a present from the South African ostrich farmers. At this time feathers were quite out of fashion and Molyneux's clever handling of them did much to make fashion-conscious people reconsider their possibilities. Photograph by Philip Harben, reproduced by courtesy of Edward Molyneux.

76 The combination of black and white is a hardy annual in all periods. Left: in 1950 Pierre Balmain used black and white spotted silk for a mid-calf slender skirt and tight-fitting bodice cinched at the waist. In 1967 Jeanne Lanvin used plain white for a free-hanging waistless dress slotted and bowed with wide black ribbons. Both models wear wide-brimmed hats, but at very different angles, one aims to appear ladylike, the other girlish. Photographs by courtesy of Pierre Balmain and Jeanne Lanvin.

77 Balenciaga's masterful handling of line and cut is exemplified in an unusual beach outfit in which bold navy and white stripes compose short pants and a high-necked pullover. The vast hat of coolie inspiration hugs the head but shades the face and shoulders. Photograph by courtesy of Tissus Abraham et Cie.

78 Above. Ungaro brought an entirely novel contribution to the fashion scene and his short skirt and short cape, both buttoned and bordered with a self-coloured edging, owe nothing to past tailoring but open a new era of constructed, rather than dressmaker-made, clothes. Drawing by Jeannette Collins, reproduced by courtesy of *The Times*.

79 Above, left. In this tailored three-piece of 1968 Nina Ricci offered a fresh interpretation of that classic, the belted Norfolk jacket, and teamed it with a short skirt, easy coat and pull-on felt hat. Photograph reproduced by courtesy of Debenham and Freebody.

80 The clothes of Italian couturiers, unlike many from their French contemporaries, tend to accentuate the feminine charm of their clients, and Valentino here exploits the seduction of white fox to make a becoming frame to the wearer's face. Coat and hat from Debenham and Freebody.

81 – 2 Hardy Amies (left) first made his name by the excellence of his tailoring, and his severe 'tailleurs', such as that shown below, enlivened by feminine falbalas and flower-trimmed hats, were in the wardrobe of every well-dressed post-war Englishwoman. Now he has expanded into the wholesale trade and his influence is world-wide, not only in women's but in men's clothes and in the accessories demanded by both sexes in a world which prefers novelty to a suit guaranteed to keep its shape for several years. Photograph by Peter Clark reproduced by courtesy of Hardy Amies.

83 – 4 When Mary Quant opened 'Bazaar' in Chelsea's King's Road in 1955 a new era opened for that neighbourhood and for English fashion. Few people have expressed the *Zeitgeist* of their time with the accuracy of this young woman who, with her husband, Alexander Plunket Greene, has had a stupendous influence on English fashion and on its overseas development. An early example of Mary's uninhibited approach to fashion is a pant-suit and shift-dress of 1963 which clearly point the way fashion has followed since that date. Photographs reproduced by courtesy of the *Daily Mirror*.

85 – 6 Two very different expressions of feminine
seduction: a Fifties version by Pierre Balmain
carried out in the richness of velvet, sables and
jewels, the body corseted, the skirt long, the hat
veiled. In 1967 the film star Julie Christie chose
to show herself to the public in this portrait by
Gerard de Rose wearing a short skirt, shirt
blouse and careless hair-do – but the verdict of
most observers was 'sexy'. Pierre Balmain
photograph by Ramon, reproduction of painting
by permission of Gerard de Rose.

imprint on his own time than any other couturier. His work bore the stamp of a real artist and his influence infiltrated every aspect of life except, of course, the kitchen, which was not then a word spoken in public or a place visited in private. But for the nursery Poiret, a most loving father, made for his children the most delightful designs both in decoration and dress.

The *fêtes* given by Poiret have passed into Parisian history and have been recorded by the brush of van Dongen, Lepape and many other artists. By 1912 Poiret had moved away from the section of Paris habitually given up to fashion and had bought a splendid *hôtel* in the Faubourg St-Honoré for his firm where he remodelled the huge garden in the style of Versailles and built a second house in it as his private residence. Here it was that he gave his famous Arabian Nights ball for which he transformed house and garden into an oriental fantasy with ibis strutting in the park, parrots in the trees, oriental dancers on the lawn, Negroes to wait on the guests while fakirs displayed their arts and Indian cooks prepared the food.

The First World War put an end to such extravagant frolics but after the armistice of 1918 he opened a house on the Rond-Point des Champs-Elysées and continued to give wonderful parties, for one of which he improvised a rubber roof to cover the entire garden to protect his guests from inclement weather. During the Exposition Décoratif of 1925 he hired three launches, called *Amour, Délices* and *Orgue,* moored near the Tuileries, on which to give mannequin parades. Alas, his taste was no longer that of the present day and certainly far from being *avant-garde.* It is an unfortunate truism that few of those involved in the development of fashion remain on the crest of the wave for more than fifteen or at the most twenty years.

Gabrielle Chanel does not reveal the date of her birth but 1883 is often quoted and, if correct, makes her the most amazing near-ninety known to fashion history. Every anecdote about this extraordinary woman is unique. She is the only couturière to retire and after an absence of sixteen years to return and offer, successfully, more or less the same line as that which made her rich and famous twenty years before. In each case she chose a moment when women were tired of the complications of *haute couture* and wished for a more active life

L

spent in less time-consuming occupations than acquiring and keeping in order an elaborate wardrobe. Chanel opened her house in Paris in 1914 but it was not until ten years later that she made her great success. In retrospect she appears, and has often been quoted as being, the sole creator of the *garçonne* girl of the 1920s which, of course, is totally untrue. Women's clothes had been shedding their extraneous tassels and trains, laces and loops for some time, and many other designers were making simpler, shorter-skirted models. What happened is what always happens when a great success occurs in any field: various circumstances combine at a certain time to help an exceptionally gifted person present his creation to the public.

Chanel had noticed during the First World War that the comfortable woollen cardigans worn by the wounded men were much envied by the women. She also learnt that a new form of knitting had been invented recently which permitted a superior type of woollen jersey to be manufactured and, with her unerring sense of contemporary taste, not the fantastic which had ruined Poiret, put two and two together and designed a collection of models with short skirts and easy cardigan jackets in good colours, beautifully cut and luxuriously finished. Woollens had never before received preferential treatment; now with crisp tailoring and such subtle touches as a tiny roll inserted in the hem to give a permanently hand-made appearance, with coquettish cuffs turned back to show the silk linings which matched the blouses or jumpers beneath, with hand-woven braid edgings and splendid jewelled buttons, the dreary jersey 'two-piece' took on a completely different aspect and entered completely different wardrobes.

One of Chanel's special signatures was a navy, brass-buttoned jacket whose scarlet lining was emphasized by its turned-back cuffs – which was a steal from a semi-naval jacket devised and worn by her friend, Jean Cocteau.

Chanel's come-back in 1954 was watched with immense interest, for her re-entry was seven years after Dior's great success with his New Look, its ladylike elegance quite unlike the casual chic of Chanel's easy suits. She has frequently voiced her boredom with her classic line, but cannot alter it any more than Worth could get rid of the crinoline; it is her individual

contribution to the fashion of her day, possibly the most
individual contribution that any couturier has yet made in this
century. Also, like Worth, Chanel attached great importance to
a particular date: she was born on 5 August, shows her summer
collection on 5 February and her winter one on 5 August and
calls her perfume Chanel No. 5.

Her life is now the subject of a full-length film, with Cecil
Beaton designing the clothes and Katharine Hepburn portraying
one of the most interesting women of her time.

While the Poiret sun sank and the Chanel sun rose an equal,
though totally different, talent came to the fore. Madeleine
Vionnet, the daughter of a tax-collector in the Jura, was born at
Aubervilliers, was married at 18, had a child who died, came to
London to learn English where she found employment in a
fashion house, but returned to Paris to accept a minor position
in the firm of Callot Soeurs. Five years later she went to
Doucet who, already ageing, wanted someone younger to inject
a spirit of youth into his collections. Here at last (she was
already 30) Vionnet was able to make her own models, only to
find them boycotted by other members of the staff. The
vendeuses, like those of a decade earlier dealing with Poiret's
designs, considered such unassuming toilettes unsuitable to the
dignity of the house. Two years later war was declared and
Vionnet did not open a house of her own until 1919, when it
was immediately successful and after only four years she was
able to buy a large house in the Avenue Matignon, where her
staff grew rapidly until, when she retired in 1939, it numbered
a thousand.

Madeleine Vionnet was more than a designer of clothes, she
was the image of her epoch but she designed for the individual
woman, not for the mass market, and undoubtedly does not
admire the low-priced, mass-produced garments which pass for
clothes today. Jacques Worth considered her the greatest
technician in the *haute couture* of her day and she was
unanimously praised as the person who introduced a new
technique into dressmaking: her bias cut had behind it a real
knowledge of construction.

Vionnet devised the method of working first on a quarter-
size wooden mannequin which gave her the figure in the round

which was essential for her cut, then when she had perfected this it was made full size in fine *toile*. From this pattern the actual material of the dress was cut. Her bias-line influenced not only all the other couturiers but all lingerie, for the *dessous* had to follow the same cross cut in order to show no seams or gathers, and perfectionists had their underwear made on the same lines as the dress it was to accompany.

During the twenty years that Vionnet had her house in the Avenue Matignon another house owned by a woman purveyed a very different but equally successful form of fashion. Jeanne Lanvin, like Madeleine Vionnet, started from the bottom and worked her way up but was already known as a great couturière before the First World War. Like Chanel, she had begun as a modiste, then had made such enchanting dresses for her little daughter that she was asked to copy them and so, step by step, she obtained a house in the Faubourg St-Honoré which was later greatly enlarged and where her grandson and his wife are now in command. On the opposite side of the road a huge building houses the men's *tailleur-chemisier* section, the perfume business is in a First Empire hotel at the Etoile and there is a branch at Cannes.

Jeanne Lanvin's signature was quite unlike Madeleine Vionnet's, yet both were typical of their time. Both carried on the long tradition of native French elegance; both catered for a *clientèle* of exceptional taste; neither used gimmicks, advertising or in any way pandered to any vulgar transitory whims; both reached the top by developing their own talents and by hard work.

Lanvin's life and work were greatly influenced by her love for her daughter, Marie-Blanche, who became the Comtesse de Polignac, and it was for this girl that she first made her 'picture dresses' at a time when clothes were far from girlish, and continued to make them all through the twenties when they were the antithesis of the short, *garçonne* mode, but her designs were so well adapted to prevailing taste that they were always wearable. Lanvin made an incomparable collection of fine paintings and particularly loved Renoir of whose work she bought many examples, and all the pictures in her collection were recognizably chosen by a woman of discriminating taste who loved colour and beauty. Her famous *bleu Lanvin* was derived from the heavenly blue of medieval church glass, she imported luxurious materials from the East and liked to make evening wraps lined with brightly coloured velvets or satins. She herself often wore a short quilted coat of some such material over another bright colour, and liked a plethora of exotic jewellery in which turquoises and corals preponderated.

Lanvin was also famous for the costumes she devised for the stage and dressed many well-known actresses, from the pre-1914 days of the great beauty Eve Lavallière (until she renounced the world and entered a convent) to Arletty and Maria Casares in the 1950s. When Yvonne Printemps went to America as Sacha Guitry's second wife she took no fewer than eighty Lanvin dresses with her. Madame Lanvin, who had already received the cross of the *Légion d'Honneur,* was chosen to represent *haute couture française* at the New York World Fair in 1939. At her death in 1945 the Comtesse de Polignac succeeded her mother as directrice and Castillo, a refugee from the Spanish War then working in America for Elizabeth Arden, was nominated designer, but he was already so well known that the firm became Lanvin-Castillo until Castillo left to open his own house, now closed.

On the male side there were three men of outstanding importance in the 1920s, two predictably French and the third yet another Englishman, the fourth of his race to compete successfully with French couturiers. Edward Molyneux had served with distinction in the First World War and won several decorations. He had had his first training with the London house of Lucille, owned by the Canadian-born Lady Duff-Gordon who brought some transatlantic verve into the London scene and set a competition for a design for an evening dress, with a job in her firm as the prize. This was won by Edward Molyneux who later, with the backing of Lord Northcliffe, owner and editor of the *Daily Mail* which gave up the front page twice a year to review his collections, opened his own house at 5 Rue de la Paix. Molyneux's collections were the delight of his customers and the despair of the journalists, for his clothes were seemingly so simple there was little to say about them except that they were exactly what was wanted.

They were devoid of exaggeration or gimmicks and remained fashionable for longer than anyone else's except Chanel's. He created clothes for the new woman who could travel extensively and the sureness of his touch surmounted differences of nationality or age. One of his most persistent trade marks was the summer suit we still wear, made of patterned silk in a timeless cut of simple jacket and pleated skirt, and another innovation which has stood the test of time was his teaming of different-coloured jackets and skirts. One of his greatest triumphs was the creation of Princess Marina's wedding dress and her entire trousseau on the occasion of her marriage to Prince George, Duke of Kent. The beauty and elegance of the bride, who had lived most of her life in Paris, made her the perfect exponent of Molyneux's reticent style, and it was noticeable that none of her coats or jackets included the stiffened-out shoulders which were then forcing their way into fashion. Molyneux chose chiefly satins and soft marocains for the Princess's evening gowns and made clever use of the ostrich plumes sent as a gift from the South African Ostrich Farmers Association.

Molyneux had wanted to be an artist and his painter's vision was manifest in his choice of colours, always soft and gradually shading, never glaring or abrupt. During times of leisure Molyneux followed his bent and painted pictures which show that had he followed this path he would have been as successful as he has been in the world of fashion. After fifteen years of retirement, which he spent mostly in the south of France, he returned to the glamour and strain of couture and, with the aid of his talented nephew, John Tullis, still works at 5 Rue de la Paix making less expensive clothes than in the old days of *haute couture* but which still have the reticence and good manners associated with his name.

Two top Frenchmen of the 1920s were Lucien Lelong and Jean Patou. The latter had made a success before 1914 but did not become famous for the easy sports clothes which were his speciality until skirts were shortened in 1924. He was particularly praised for his tennis costumes and Suzanne Lenglen, who wore his clothes both on and off the court, did much to popularize the pull-over and pleated skirt which

became (and still is) a uniform for young women. In the six
years after he reopened in the Rue St-Florentin in 1918 his
turnover increased twenty-four times. In those days the role of
mannequin was not considered enviable and no girl from a good
background would undertake such a job, but Patou had
noticed that the American social order was quite unlike the
European and conceived the idea of getting some attractive
young Americans to show off his sports clothes which the
Paris mannequins were not used to wearing and consequently
wore badly. He approached the *doyenne* of American fashion,
Mrs Edna Woolman Chase, editor-in-chief of *Vogue,* and she
helped him to select six girls who were widely publicized as the
six most elegant models in the world. Certainly nothing like
them had been seen before in the Paris fashion world and their
vitality and casual chic made a tremendous impression. Not
only were these girls beautiful and elegant but they were also
socially presentable and soon they, and the Patou clothes, were
seen to their best advantage at every fashionable occasion in
France.

Lucien Lelong, whose parents had a small fashion house
before the war, set up his own house in 1919 and five years
later moved to the Avenue Matignon where he employed 1,200
workers. He will always be remembered for two major
contributions to fashion: he was the first to launch a ready-made
department and for his *robes d'édition,* as he called them, had a
large room decorated in stark white by Jean Michel-Frank in
1933, thus antedating the Courrèges simple setting by thirty
years. His other innovation was that of making his openings
similar to a private theatre party with his lovely wife, Princess
Natalie Paley, later Mrs John Wilson, receiving the guests who
were seated in rows in the long salon, which had a stage at one
end where the mannequins posed before walking down the aisle
among the audience.

In the 1930s a great change came over the French fashion
scene. Not only did the crash of the American stock market
seriously affect the couture houses but the supremacy which
hitherto the French had exercised over fashion was now
challenged. Up to the middle of the 1920s all the names of the
couturiers had been French: Doucet, Doeuillet, Poiret, Cheruit,

Lanvin, Chanel, Vionnet, Worth (grandson of the founder and thoroughly French): now a group of international figures entered the hitherto exclusively French domain. The English Molyneux was the first to infiltrate in the late 1920s, then came Schiaparelli, Italian; Mainbocher, American; Robert Piguet, Swiss; Maggy Rouff, Belgian; Balenciaga, Spanish. Of them all only Balenciaga and Schiaparelli made truly original contributions to fashion.

Elsa Schiaparelli, the child of an Italian professor of oriental languages, had a difficult beginning in life which included an unfortunate marriage (in London) to a Polish dreamer who took her to America, spent her dowry and left her with a child. She began to make a living in Paris by designing sweaters patterned with Negro or tattooist motifs which she persuaded Armenian refugees to knit for her. They were an immediate success and one of her first customers was Anita Loos, whose book *Gentlemen Prefer Blondes* was an international bestseller (both she and 'Scap' are brunettes). 'Scap' took four little rooms on the top floor of a house in the Rue de la Paix, decorated them in the bleak black and white formula then fashionable, and was soon turning out 8,000 dresses a year and dressing Greta Garbo. Her clothes were never pretty nor were they good clothes for pretty women, but of these there are few and it was the many plain ones who benefited by the *panache* of her models.

'Scap's' great success was the manner in which she developed the size of the shoulders in order to diminish the waist. The flat-breasted days of the 1920s were over, bosoms were appearing again and her clever cut squared the shoulders, slightly rounded the bosom and whittled away the waist. Her other great contribution was the tweed suit which she transformed from a colourless utility coverage into an enviable and dashing costume. To a sound basic cut she added a mass of inventive detail and became known for her original trimmings and buttons, and for the intelligent use to which she put the marvellous tweeds woven specially for her by the Macleods of Skye which were worlds away from the conservative woollens previously considered correct for the country.

'Scap's' collections were always built around a theme: one

season it was the circus, at another butterflies or Botticelli gave her her inspiration. Her openings were as eagerly awaited as a first night and attended by as many of 'tout Paris' as could be accommodated in her new premises in the Place Vendôme (the very house where Madame Cheruit was established many years before).

On the ground floor an Aladdin's cave of novelties was supervised by a decorative American girl with the plain name of Bettina Jones (now Madame Gaston Bergerie), whose charm was only equalled by her ingenuity and who made this small entrance a meeting-place for smart Parisiennes and the international set. Many of Schiaparelli's novelties would now be called psychedelic, for she had handbags which lit up inside and phosphorescent jewellery which glowed in the dark. In this field she had the collaboration of some of the most brilliant young artists in Paris and Jean Schlumberger, now a famous New York jeweller, designed some of her costume jewellery. She developed materials from newsprint collages, brought back burnouses from Africa and transformed them into magnificent evening wraps, copied embroideries from Russia and Peru, and called her perfume Shocking Pink from a design made for her by Christian Bérard.

Another woman of a very different character and taste appeared in the early 1930s and is still in business, selling remakes of the styles which astonished Paris in 1932. Of all the couturiers Madame Grès has the most personal style, firmly founded on her love and knowledge of classical sculpture. When Mademoiselle Alix, as she was first called, showed some of her sketches to Michel de Brunhof and hesitantly asked his advice, the distinguished editor of French *Vogue* replied that she had better forget couture and continue with her sculpture. Later, when he saw her first collection, with that generosity which characterized him, he immediately recognized her unusual talent and devoted a double spread in *Vogue* to announce to the fashion world that a new talent had been born. Madame Grès cuts the material herself and her technique is so much part of her style that no one has ever been able to copy her. She trains a few girls but she alone designs and is responsible for the hundreds of models she shows each year. Her draped dresses are *chefs-d'oeuvres* which often use twenty yards of clinging silk jersey and may take a month to drape, mould and sew into the myriad folds which must take and follow the human form. Like Poiret, she forbids corsets and ignores bosoms and will not dress anyone who has a trimly upholstered figure, scorning all reinforcements such as the built-in bras and waspies which made Dior's dresses an easy way of dressing. But to those who have tall figures and personal elegance, such as Nancy Mitford who is one of her most faithful clients, her clothes are investments rather than coverage. They are outside the usual run of fashion but bridge the decades so easily that Marlene Dietrich's daughter wore with *éclat* a dress which Madame Grès had made for her mother twenty years earlier.

Mainbocher, whose name was originally Main Bocher, was a mid-Westerner who came to Europe to study music and then art, became fashion editor of *Vogue* in Paris, where his observant eye summed up and reported the fashion scene with unusual acumen. Soon he decided to create fashions rather than report them and set up in the Avenue George V, which he decorated with the same quiet good taste that characterized his clothes. At the outbreak of war in 1939 he closed the house in Paris and opened in New York, where he is still active and numbers among his customers the Duchess of Windsor, whose wedding costume he made.

The firm of Heim was a feature of the Paris fashion scene before the First World War, for the family were furriers and it was the mother of the present Jacques Heim who in 1919 suggested to Chanel that rabbit skins, if used with taste and originality, might make a contribution to *haute couture*, then short of both furs and fabrics. Chanel lined her loose easy-to-wear coats in rabbit dyed unexpected colours and continues to do so today. Heim was one of the several Paris houses which had branches in pre-war London: the first was Poiret who in the 1920s had a house at 7 Albemarle Street, followed by Worth who had a speciality shop for sports clothes in Regent Street, and in the 1930s Schiaparelli, Piguet and Maggy Rouff all had salons in London until the war closed them.

During the war the *haute couture* in Paris carried on in a

greatly diminished form, guided by Lucien Lelong who as
head of the Syndicat de la Couture endeavoured to keep a
nucleus of this great national industry alive.

The post-war scene was strikingly unlike the pre-war. It was
now completely male-dominated: Chanel was in retirement,
Grès went her own way unswayed by passing events. It also
was once again predominantly French. There were Lucien
Lelong, Jacques Fath, Marcel Rochas, Nina Ricci (originally
Italian but now directed by her French son) and later there
were Jacques Griffe, Guy Laroche, Balmain, Dior, Givenchy,
with the only foreign exceptions the Greek Jean Dessès, the
Spanish Castillo at Lanvin and, towering above all, Cristobal
Balenciaga.

A great loss to French couture was the early death of Jacques
Fath, whose *fêtes* were modest perhaps compared with Poiret's
but were the highlight of the post-war fashion scene. In the
summer the first presentation of the collection was shown at
night in the large floodlit tree-shaded courtyard of his house in
the Rue Pierre Ier de Serbie, with all his guests in dazzling
evening gowns and champagne flowing. On Sundays he would
invite a select few of the most important buyers and journalists
to his country house. His clothes were like himself: ebullient,
showy, good-humoured and great fun, and it was in his salons
that the lovely red-haired Bettina, later associated with Aly
Khan, made her first appearance.

Marcel Rochas was another gay extrovert who loved parties,
people and pretty women and immediately after the war,
together with his third wife, became associated with the very
feminine type of clothes she liked to wear. He was one of the
several couturiers who insisted that *they* were the pre-war
instigators of the *guêpière*, or wasp-waisted corset which became
an essential post-war accessory. Rochas was fascinated by the
cinema and designed many costumes for film stars, and in
Jacques Becker's film *Falbalas* he played the part of Bluebeard
who hung up in a shop window all the women he had loved
in the dresses he had made for them. He died in 1953, still
young, having enjoyed his life to the end.

Lelong's great contribution to the post-war scene was that he
gave positions as designers to two young men who were

destined to influence the whole course of fashion, Pierre
Balmain and Christian Dior. The latter was a young man born
in diplomatic circles, who had previously been an art dealer but
had been obliged to close his shop in 1939. Now in 1946 he was
made responsible for the major part of Lelong's first post-war
collection, which was an unprecedented success. Customers from
abroad, of course, had no idea of who was behind the scenes
as the creative spirit and at a dinner party an English
journalist, finding herself beside a quiet little man with rather
a pink face and delicate hands, overjoyed to be once again in
the Paris she had known and loved all her life, spoke with
enthusiasm of the lovely clothes she had seen that afternoon at
Lelong's, so subtle, distinguished and simple, yet so new and
fresh. The little pink man got pinker and said not without
emotion that he was pleased to hear such an opinion since he
was the designer, and that his name was Christian Dior. Not
long after the success of this collection Christian Dior met
Monsieur Boussac, the great textile industrialist, who told him
he intended to organize a retail outlet for his materials, with
the result that Boussac set up Christian Dior in magnificent
premises in the Avenue Matignon where, behind a façade of
great luxury, a business organization was built such as no
couture house had ever had before, where records were kept
with the computer-like efficiency that only a self-made
millionaire could impose on such an individual affair as fashion.
This meant that Dior never had any financial or domestic
worries (though of course if he had not 'delivered the goods'
the house and all its trappings would have vanished like a
dream); with Boussac's support he was able to gather round
him some of the most distinguished people of his day to help
him develop a business which grew at an astonishing rate. The
house of Dior began in 1947 with one company, three
workrooms and eighty-five hands; only six years later it
consisted of six companies, sixteen associated enterprises spread
all over the world, twenty-eight workrooms and over 1,000
workers. In 1958 Dior sold more than half as much as all the
other couturiers in Paris put together, 50 per cent of its
business with private customers, and the rest with foreign
buyers.

Lucien Lelong, who behaved with the good manners that had made him the popular president for many years of the Chambre Syndicale de la Couture and enabled him to deal successfully with the German forces of occupation, attended Dior's first collection where the New Look was born and embraced and complimented his ex-designer on a collection which made French fashion history and altered the shape of women all over the world.

After Dior's early and unexpected death Yves St-Laurent was given the greatly coveted position of head designer to the house, but later founded a house of his own, and Marc Bohan, late of Patou, is now the responsible head.

Jean-Jacques Crahay, now the designer at Lanvin's, like Lucien Lelong and Jacques Heim, was born in *chiffons*. His family had a dressmaking business in Liège so he went through the routine of training, entered a technical college to take a course in pattern drawing and cutting but was shortly afterwards mobilized, taken prisoner and remained in captivity for five years. When he returned to civilian life he reorganized the family dressmaking business in Liège but left it to go into partnership with Germaine de Vilmorin. Later he became designer for Nina Ricci, where he worked until Monsieur and Madame Yves Lanvin asked him to become artistic director to the house of Jeanne Lanvin.

Pierre Balmain had originally wished to be an architect but interrupted his studies to work at Molyneux where he spent five years. In 1939 he was mobilized and sent to Savoy, where he met and made friends with Gertrude Stein who, a vast black-clad woman in sandals, attended all his collections until her death in 1946.

In 1945 Balmain opened his own *maison de couture* in the Rue François Ier and in the following year, sponsored by Gertrude Stein, gave a lecture tour in America to women's colleges and universities. A later visit to the Far East resulted in his dressing the exquisitely beautiful Queen of Thailand.

Hubert Givenchy began his career in the boutique of Schiaparelli and had also worked with Fath, Piguet and Lelong before he decided to start his own. His resources were limited and he furnished his salon economically with two rows of

canvas-covered chairs and some amusing figurines decked
out with novelties. He had not the funds to buy beautiful silks
or expensive woollens, nor would the manufacturers offer him,
as they do to well-established firms, sample lengths which they
hope will launch a vogue for a certain type of cloth or shade
of colour. He showed to a curious but sceptical press a
collection entirely made of inexpensive cottons which was an
instantaneous success. He had one trump card in his hand: he
had persuaded Bettina, Jacques Fath's head model and one of
the most popular girls in Paris, to leave Fath, and this charming
redhead, whose every entrance seemed to bring fresh air into
the hot-house atmosphere of a Paris salon, electrified the bored
buyers perched on uncomfortable chairs. The full skirts of
striped shirting and cambric blouses with elaborate frillings that
Givenchy designed for her made immediate fashion history and
were *the* fashion for the next summer. Later his friendship with
Balenciaga greatly influenced him; his tailoring improved and
the scope of his collections widened. But no one who witnessed
his *début* in that mock François Ier house overlooking the Parc
Monceau with the pretty Bettina flashing in and out in her full
skirts and frilly blouses will ever forget it.

Cristobal Balenciaga, for so long the *éminence grise* of couture,
was born in a Spanish seaside town where his father was
captain of a fishing vessel. When he was only a boy he saw a
smart woman in the little resort wearing a beautifully cut
costume and asked if he could copy it. She thought this
merely a joke but lent it to him and he returned it with a
perfect twin. Balenciaga left Spain at the time of the Spanish
Civil War and in 1936 came to London to look for a job,
applied to some of the court dressmakers and to one of the
large Oxford Street stores, but failed and returned disheartened
to Paris, where with the help of a friend, Monsieur de
Latinville, he opened his own salon on the Avenue George V.
It is fascinating to speculate what would have been the result
if Balenciaga had found work in London – would he have
evolved as he did, or would he have been frustrated by the
insular prejudices of England and the lack of adequate support
in the workroom? He alone of all the couturiers knew how to
cut and stitch every part of a garment, he was a perfectionist

and all his clothes bore the imprint of his ordered mind and skilful fingers. He was also alone among the couturiers in avoiding all publicity; few people ever saw him, let alone met him. He never appeared in his own salons, never gave parties or interviews and to be invited into his book-lined study was a rare compliment. He never marketed all the fringe attractions of the fashion game, styled no stockings or shoes though he marketed a perfume which like his clothes was extremely expensive, but there was no alluring boutique on the ground floor of his house.

He had a branch of his business in Madrid under the name of Aissa but no subsidiary companies dealing with the ready-to-wear. He refused to accommodate the dates of his collections to suit the Chambre Syndicale and forced the journalists to return to Paris weeks later to see his collection only and later that of his disciple, Givenchy. He put every difficulty in the path of the buyers, asking a deposit of £1,000 before they were allowed to enter, and was selective not only about the types of clothes and materials which he showed but also about whom he dressed. When he retired in 1968 an epoch ended; he was the last of the great couturiers founded on aristocratic chic, not youth.

Three newcomers, Pierre Cardin, Courrèges and Ungaro, all made their success in their twenties, a new departure for the world of couture in which previously most would-be designers worked several years with other couture houses before opening on their own though this early success, a phenomenon of the last twenty years, is not surprising in a world dedicated to youth. Far more surprising is that after Schiaparelli closed her house in 1950 no woman designer of any importance has emerged. Women have at last found a place in most professions and after a war in which for the first time (since the legendary Amazons) they had been closely involved, and in France had done inestimable work in the Resistance in which some had lost their lives, they continued to have little to say in what they wore.

Before the First World War there had been the elegant Mesdames Cheruit and Paquin and the Callot sisters, and before them Palmyre and Victorine; in the eighteenth century,

Rose Bertin and Mademoiselle Pagelle. The men who succeeded these feminine creators all had deep sentimental attachments to women, Doucet to an adored unknown, Worth and Poiret both had beautiful wives whom they delighted to dress, while Patou's conquests were almost as many and as varied as his collections. After the war a group of confirmed bachelors took over and of the entire world couture only Marcel Rochas and Jacques Fath were married, and of the succeeding generation only Louis Féraud entered into matrimony and then with none other than the lovely Mia Fonssagrives, daughter of one of the most beautiful pre-war models whose face smiles out of dozens of *Vogue* photographs of the 1930s.

7 The English scene

In England the fashion picture has always been strikingly different from that of Paris. There were no famous dressmakers in the eighteenth and nineteenth centuries and no creative designers among the so-called court dressmakers of the early years of this century. Reville was the key-name in English fashion and dressmaker to Queen Mary, but he had no personal style internationally known, as had his rival Poiret. His forte was the formal toilette essential for court receptions and the races and his large salons in Hanover Square, where now stands the Dolcis shoe-shop, was a temple of discreet luxury. All was grey, soft and impressive and the furniture, of course, Louis XV. Customers, who arrived in their cars accompanied by chauffeurs and footmen, were received as visitors, treated with the greatest respect and shown coloured sketches of the models proposed for the season, together with some made-up examples worn by the tall model girls who wandered about in his 'creations', holding in the right hand a tall Regency walking stick, which Reville considered gave them an air of elegance and improved their stance. No two ladies would be given exactly the same gown, for nearly all Reville's customers went to the same court functions, so, as it was not possible to make two dresses alike, special suggestions or alterations were made to the original sketches, new sketches produced, until the client and the *vendeuse* agreed on exact lines, materials and, above all, on trimmings – on the laces, ruches, flounces, tassels and embroideries which then played a dominant role. Already in the 1920s Reville was out of date, Chanel and the style she stood for had ended his reign, but for a time Reville was joined by Rossiter and later the firm was merged with that of the London Worth; Reville himself was unable to adjust to a changing world and he died alone and in want.

Across Hanover Square, in the building now called Celanese House, were the salons of Lucille (Lady Duff Gordon) where the models were more exotic than at Reville's, and Lucille's head mannequin, Margot, was the first to become a personally known photographic model.

Madame Handley-Seymour was the most important of the court dressmakers and made the coronation dress of the Duchess of York when she became queen. Although there were several other smaller firms which specialized in the 'tea-gown' fashion life veered in a different direction as cocktails replaced tea and the cocktail dress the *négligée*. English tailor-mades continued to be cut and fitted expertly, but fashionable gowns were copies of Paris models.

London produced no indigenous group of fashion designers, nor any recognized school of training. Girls were taken on as apprentices but the standard of work and the facilities for all the falbalas which go to make up fashion were lacking in England, and Molyneux preferred to take the enormous risk of setting up in Paris rather than face the conditions of the fashion trade in London.

So when in the 1930s a world-wide financial crisis and home unemployment forced the fashion industry to try to promote English fashions, talent was scarce. An embryo group of designers, strongly individualistic people, greatly aided by the press, formed a fashion group affiliated to the Fashion Group of America, held meetings between designers and manufacturers, attempted to co-ordinate press releases with the dates of the collections and generally helped to organize the fashion market.

First and foremost among these designers was Norman Hartnell, who in the early 1920s abandoned his study of architecture at Cambridge to become a dress designer. He was

responsible for the costumes for a university theatrical
performance which caught the eye of Miss Minnie Hogg,
whose daily column in the *Evening Standard* under the
pseudonym of Corisande was read by every London woman.
She predicted a great future for the amateur artist, and fired by
this praise Hartnell decided to follow his bent and become a
dress designer. The field seemed wide open, most houses
copied French models and no one considered the Englishwoman,
except Lucille and the ageing Mr Reville who himself took his
designs to Buckingham Palace for the approval of Queen Mary
and King George V, who was most particular about the
Queen's attire.

Hartnell tells ruefully but amusingly in his book *The Silver
and the Gold* the story of his early attempts: no one would even
look at his sketches except Lucille, who pirated them and
passed them off as her own, his first job at £3 a week lasted
only a couple of months and he was fired just before Christmas.
Finally with £300 and a devoted sister but with no experience
either of book-keeping or dressmaking he set up for himself in
four small rooms at the top of a house in Bruton Street. His
first success came when, at a collection described as 'witty as a
Firbank novel', the Hon. Daphne Vivian, one of the loveliest
girls of her day, chose a sensational gold and silver dress for
her wedding to the Marquess of Bath. Everyone knows the
development of this success story. By the early 1930s Hartnell
was installed in a splendid house in Bruton Street where in a
pale almond green drawing-room lined with mirrors he
displayed his dresses on mannequins who became famous
names. His establishment still is the largest English couture
house and the only one with its own embroidery room.
World-wide fame came when Lady Alice Montagu-Douglas-
Scott on the occasion of her marriage to the Duke of Gloucester
ordered from him her wedding gown and those of her
bridesmaids among whom were two children, the nieces of the
bridegroom, daughters of the Duke and Duchess of York, now
respectively Her Majesty Queen Elizabeth II and Princess
Margaret, Countess of Snowdon. Splendid though this
occasion was, it was nothing to what lay ahead, for with the
accession of the Duke and Duchess of York to the throne it

was Norman Hartnell who took his sketches and his fitters to the Palace for the coronation robes, as he still does for the present Queen, as well as remaining the couturier of the Queen Mother. One of his outstanding successes was the manner in which he solved the problem of the exacting wardrobe demanded by a royal visit to Paris after the Duchess of York had become Queen. With the death of George V so recent bright colours were out of the question but so was unrelieved black. Hartnell recalled that the queens of France when in mourning always dressed in white and therefore made all the Queen's reception and evening gowns in white lace, tulle or satin, which made a great impression on the Parisians. Hartnell's coronation dress for the present Queen was a masterpiece of design and execution, embroidered with the symbols of England, Scotland, Ireland and Wales, the rose, thistle, shamrock and leek, which gained world-wide praise.

As well as creating the most elaborate dresses for such ceremonial occasions Hartnell also became the first couturier to work for the mass-production of inexpensive dresses and was associated with the firm of Berkertex as early as 1946.

Hartnell now has an advisory position with the enormously influential Great Universal Stores which sell throughout the country, and has recently entered the field of masculine fashion. He travels extensively developing his many-sided business which includes stockings, jewellery, perfume, and read-to-wear clothes, to promote which he has opened a boutique in his Bruton Street premises and another in Glasgow.

Victor Stiebel, who came from South Africa, also intended to study architecture at Cambridge and again, like Hartnell, designed some costumes for a theatrical production. So good were they, and so delighted was he by the work, that he too decided he would become a dress designer. His parents thought otherwise but he managed to obtain some capital and opened in Bruton Street, a few doors from Hartnell but in a far simpler décor.

A few other designers of native talent appeared. An Irishman called Digby Morton attracted the attention of the fashion journalists by making tweed suits which were not in the usual dowdy shapes and muddy shades but, though cut with dash and in clear colours, were eminently suited for country-house wear. He also took rooms in Bruton Street, which looked as if it were about to become the Rue de la Paix of London.

From an even more unlikely source than Ireland a delightfully eccentric character who had spent most of his life on horse-back in India now began to design women's dresses. This was Peter Russell, who evolved a very personal style and managed fabric manufacturers as well as he had horses in his earlier years.

Another arrival, and the only woman in this new world of London fashion, was Elspeth Champcommunal, who was asked to design for the house of Reville, now amalgamated with the London branch of Worth. She had had a small but supremely elegant fashion house of her own in Paris, in which the walls were decorated by Pedro Pruna, then an artist very much in vogue, but this was a casualty of the American market collapse as her capital came mainly from the United States. With exquisite taste, particularly in colours, for she originally had gone to Paris to study painting, she was a welcome addition to this nucleus of indigenous dress designers in London.

In a Mayfair mews there was a small house which had great influence on English fashion. Lachasse was a modest establishment chiefly concerned with tailoring, owned by Mr Singleton, the husband of 'Miss Grey', one of the best known of the court dressmakers. This was the nursery where Digby Morton had his training and, when he left Lachasse to strike out on his own, he was obliged by the terms of his contract to set up his premises two miles away from Mayfair for at least two years, which meant the desolation of Queens Gate. No one thought women would go so far to buy a suit but they were proved wrong, and in due course Digby Morton returned to the West End.

To replace Digby Morton at Lachasse Mr Singleton engaged a young man whose chief qualifications seemed to be that he was a keen and successful seller of weighing machines, and spoke German fluently, but he also appeared remarkably well informed in matters of fashion (his mother was a *vendeuse* at Miss Grey's). Hardy Amies made an immediate success by his fresh approach to tailoring but in later years he has developed a more varied style and has now become the 'grand mogul' of

fashion in England. At his collection in the summer of 1939,
only a few weeks before war broke out, he opened the show
with three girls dressed in nothing but tiny pink satin corsets
and flounced petticoats; then, having made his point that
waists were in and petticoats should support skirts, he showed
a delightful collection of young clothes which incorporated
these two new features. Only too soon his knowledge of
German was of more use than his fashion flair and he was in
uniform, and did not return to civilian life until 1946. He set
up his own establishment at 14 Savile Row, a fine Georgian
house with panelled rooms where Sheridan had lived and
died.

Hardy Amies now holds the appointment of Dressmaker to
the Queen, was elected a member of the faculty of Royal
Designers for Industry, and has won innumerable awards. But
what really rates him high in the fashion world is that he has
entered and succeeded in two widely different fields of mass-
production, and is responsible for a vast output of both men's
and women's fashions, and more than thirty-three firms in
Britain and the Commonwealth manufacture under licence his
designs for every form of garment worn by man and woman.

The world-wide success of the Amies venture is a far cry
from his early career, particularly from the meticulous tailoring
of which his house produced outstanding examples until more
feminine lines ousted the impeccable man-tailored suits which
held their shape for several seasons. Amies still shows a couture
collection twice a year for those clients whose figures are
difficult but their purses easy, and caters for many of the most
elegant women in England. Some of the Queen's most
successful outfits, particularly during the tour in India, were of
Amies' making. These couture collections are bolstered by a
well-stocked ready-to-wear boutique where his feeling for good
taste quietly persists.

In 1942 the Incorporated Society of London Fashion
Designers was formed. The Society followed much the same
procedure as the Paris Syndicat de la Couture, although on a
smaller scale: it organized the various fashion shows so that
none of them overlapped, arranged that the London collections
were shown a week before Paris so there could be no question

of copying, publicized the dates and times when the different
houses presented their collections and acted as hosts to foreign
buyers. The Incorporated Society's first president was the
elegant Hon. Mrs 'Reggie' Fellowes, who brought her
knowledge of the international market and influence to help
this new group struggling with the difficulties of war-time
production, which made exports an even more important
matter than in the 1930s. Mrs Fellowes was followed by
Edward Molyneux, who after the war continued to make his
headquarters in London, and in the 1950s several new names
were added to the Society, most eminent among them Michael,
the only English house to achieve a truly international signature.
Norman Hartnell was the next president of the Society which
did an outstanding job in persuading the rest of the world,
particularly America whose dollars England needed so badly,
of the existence of a real English couture different from,
though equal in quality to, the French. The brilliant Lady
Pamela Berry, now Lady Hartwell, daughter of the great F. E.
Smith, was the enthusiastic leader of the 'Inc-Soc', as the
Society was generally known, until its near collapse in the early
1960s. In 1969 only four of the 'Big Ten' (who were once
eleven) showed to a shrinking couture-minded public.

The development which was to put English fashion on the
international map was a far cry from the well-tailored and
ladylike garments which were the pride of the Incorporated
Society. In 1955 a girl called Mary Quant, after completing a
course of fashion design at a suburban school of art, obtained
a position stitching millinery in a basement which brought her
£2 10s. a week. Shortly afterwards she married a young man,
Alexander Plunket Greene, who was able to find a small
capital which they thought, though no one else would have
agreed, was sufficient to start a business. They opened a small
shop in the King's Road with clothes designed and cut by Mary
and made by a few kindly Italians in her sitting-room. Only
later did the young enthusiasts learn they had broken practically
every licensing rule and the terms of their lease, but by then such
small items were forgotten in a deluge of publicity – unsought –
and in one of the most extraordinary developments in English
fashion. Mary not only has a real flair for design but a husband,

unlike most, who realizes what she wants to do and be,
and a third member of her team, Archie McNeil, who
understands finance and somehow kept them afloat during the
first eight years when the business was expanding at such a
rate and size that they never had any money. From making
100 dresses a month they suddenly jumped to 10,000 with no
capital to pay for the material and the workers – now they
draw royalties of over £4 million a year on dresses alone.

Mary is one of those fortunate people who belong properly
in their own period, in the telling French phrase *elle est bien
dans son assiette* and, comfortably secure in the plate of her time,
she looks neither backwards nor forwards but faces the present.
The make-believe of couture and high-fashion she neither
considers nor condemns; it is not for her or for the tens of
thousands of young women all over the world who realize
that she speaks the language of their youth. She expresses the
spirit of her time with an accuracy seldom vouchsafed to those
who wish by whatever means, painting, writing or designing,
to record and enrich their age. She wants to have things
manufactured as easily and cheaply as possible and instead of
making useless efforts to try to put back the clock she likes
machinery because it saves girls (like her) stitching in a
basement for an inadequate wage to make one hat for one
woman to wear one day at Ascot. She wants aesthetics to
combine with mechanical ingenuity and likes to be presented
with problems which demand such a union.

Her success is stupendous. She not only produces
twenty-eight collections a year but has them in many countries.
In 1967 she exported 30,000 dresses to France alone, she has big
markets all over Europe and a tie-up in America which took
her there eighteen times in a year. Her 'Ginger Group', born in
1964, kept her and Alexander awake at night with worry, but
didn't prevent them flying somewhere almost every week to follow
the jet-speed of the Group's success. She has given furs a new
dimension, perched a beret at a new angle, experimented with
moulded plastics until she has given shoes a new way of
walking and coats a new shape. A whole generation of girls
looks different, feels different, and thinks differently because
this young woman found her right place at the right time.

Everyone recognized that here was a talent which spoke clearly for the 'here and now' and in June 1966 in the Queen's Birthday Honours List she was given the O.B.E. for her services to export.

Now the fashion scene has changed again and the English market, once associated with well-tailored suits or sensible clothes, is noticeable for the fantastic and highly original work of Zandra Rhodes. This young girl with her free-wheeling methods has successfully launched her expensive, hand-made dresses carried out in elaborately patterned materials of her own devising, not only in England but across the Channel and the Atlantic. Zandra's clothes have an air of drama, never a characteristic of Britain's fashions but perhaps part of the uninhibited self-expression to be found in all sections of the arts in England today. They also represent a much overdue and refreshing return to a world of beautiful make-believe and a poetical rather than a practical approach to body-covering.

8 Ready-made clothes

Ready-made clothes are far from being an invention of the twentieth century. In England 200 years ago there was a large ready-made trade, especially in children's clothes, and sharp rivalry between the clothiers of Monmouth Street who sold cheap second-hand suits and the merchants of Birchin Lane who boasted they could supply new goods at the same price.

In eighteenth-century Paris a few percipient dealers in cast-off garments had the bright idea of approaching dressmakers and tailors for the clothes which had not pleased their clients and sold these at the Marché St-Jacques, which in the 1790s became the centre of this new form of ready-made clothes, known as *dix-huit* because they were *deux fois neuf*.

In time this hazardous street-hawking became a respectable business, backed by a group of textile manufacturers who saw in it a new and large outlet for their goods. In 1824 the first house in which ready-made clothes of good quality were sold was opened, called La Jardinière because it was close to the flower market. Social conditions were changing fast; there was now a new middle class which demanded to be well dressed, not in a manner reminiscent of the despised aristocrats of the past but like men of the future, businessmen and industrialists.

Soon many producers of ready-made clothes appeared and only twenty years later (1844) there were already 225 such businesses in France. A new kind of specialist appeared,

someone who knew about buying material wholesale, how to
cut it by machine and either put it together in his own
workrooms or give it to outworkers. In the meantime a new
element had entered the fashion scene which radically
altered methods of dressmaking and offered vast possibilities.
In 1830 an unknown engineer in the Rhône Valley invented a
machine which he wanted to sell in Paris. He was so poor he
walked all the way to the capital carrying his precious
invention in a sack, which contained the prototype of the
sewing machine. Thimmonnier died poor and unknown, and it
was only later that the American Singer developed this machine,
made a fortune from it, and married his daughter to a French
duke.

With this aid to quick construction the ready-made clothing
industry developed rapidly, chiefly in America where vast
distances made it difficult for people to get to shops, where it
was unlikely that any one woman would see another in the
same dress – something which does not worry the young
today but which was considered disastrous by well-dressed
women before the last war – and where the local dressmakers
who made by hand in Europe were unknown. This fascinating
market is a field of study too large to be attempted here but it
is worth while remembering that it had a fifty-year start on the
European ready-to-wear which did not enter the high-fashion
world until after the Second World War when, helped by the
decline of snobbery, the loss of the 'little woman round the
corner' who made to measure and the increase in the number
of women who work, ready-made clothes began to attract
some of the best designers in the country.

The wholesale fashion trade in England made an
enormous post-war effort to extend its exports and to create a
high-fashion image instead of the bread-and-butter style
previously associated with off-the-peg clothes. In 1947 fourteen
of the best ready-to-wear firms formed the Model House Group,
later developed into the Fashion House Group of London, which
included twenty-seven manufacturers and twenty-four associate
members dealing with accessories, and put on professional dress
shows of high quality. Under the able chairmanship of
Frederick Starke and the aegis of the Board of Trade were

carried out successfully such ambitious projects as a fashion show on the Cunarder *Queen Elizabeth*, which startled New York with its first-ever mini-skirts, white stockings and neo-Victorian bloomers.

In 1963 a council for men's wear was formed, and in 1966 the Clothing Export Council was organized, led by the dynamic Mr Abraham of Aquascutum, to act as a clearing house for all the related groups, including those dealing with children's clothes plus the old-established Wholesale Fashion Trades Association, now entitled the Apparel and Fashion Industries. A twice-yearly Fashion Buyers Diary is brought out which schedules the many shows of the wholesale trade in all its aspects and which are attended in the spring and autumn by hundreds of buyers from all over the world.

Although English 'ready-mades' do not yet rate the high prices of American top models where originals by Norman Norell and Galanos of New York can cost £500 or more, they can still be taken off the peg for over £200 in several fashion-conscious English stores.

The precision in sizing, the expertise in copying good models have recently resulted in major changes in the shopping habits of the Londoner. Several stores have each 'bought' a Paris designer of top rank and copied his models seam for seam, button for button, in a range of accepted sizes: Courrèges at Harrods, Ungaro at Fortnum & Mason, Philippe Venet at Selfridges, and a choice of top French and Italian names at Debenham's. For some time Christian Dior has run his own boutique in Conduit Street. In the past a French model was 'adapted' to the client's liking, with the result that she wore a hybrid garment instead of a model and never appeared correctly dressed; now she can buy in her own size an exact reproduction, at a staggering difference in price averaging about a quarter of what the clothes would cost made to order in their Parisian settings.

Another great change in fashion shopping is the proliferation of 'boutiques', small shops run by individuals whose taste influences the wholesalers from whom they buy but who chiefly rely on a small number of copies of their own designs, made by small firms. This allows for a constantly changing stock and, together with the geographical realignment of the London shopping area which has broken down the mystique of Mayfair, permits girls, all with pay packets in their hands, to buy quickly and cheaply in their own neighbourhood where the small boutiques evolve a special type which suits their known customers.

Today the immensely complicated machinery which co-ordinates the interests of textile and dress manufacturers, publicity and press forces the pace of fashion at a rate unimaginable a couple of decades ago, and each season presents new ideas which are as wide in their distribution as they are limited in their duration. Any novelty is considered becoming until its freshness fades, when it is harshly criticized, and any on-coming fashion is thought beautiful since it not only affords a relief from what went before but holds the warrant of contemporary approval. The principle of novelty in conjunction with the law of conspicuous waste is an unfailing stimulus for fashion.

The recent vogue for the anti-pretty swept away the womanly-woman of the 1950s; men's and women's clothes now resemble each other so closely that one would be inclined to believe, if evidence did not prove the contrary, that companionate rather than sexual marriage was the aim of the young.

Together with the levelling-out process which has diminished the contrast between the sexes, the rich and the poor, the young and the old, has gone the breaking down of the seasons. Time was when summer meant putting on white and light-coloured clothing; now man-made miracle fibres permit these to be worn all the year round, jet travel has confused our sense of time and place, sex differences are less distinct, the seasons scrambled. . . . Is it loss or gain?

Index